EFFECTIVE CORPORATE GOVERNANCE

Theory and Best Practices

Kirimi Barine

David Minja

Series in Business and Finance

VERNON PRESS

In the Americas:
Vernon Press
1000 N West Street, Suite 1200,
Wilmington, Delaware 19801
United States

In the rest of the world:
Vernon Press
C/Sancti Espiritu 17,
Malaga, 29006
Spain

Series in Business and Finance

Library of Congress Control Number: 2022946417

ISBN: 978-1-64889-725-2

Also available: 978-1-64889-531-9 [Hardback]; 978-1-64889-665-1 [PDF, E-Book]

Cover design by Vernon Press. Cover image designed by kjpargeter / Freepik.

To the students, practitioners and experts of Leadership and governance.

Table of Contents

Acknowledgements

WRITING A BOOK is rewarding in more ways than you can imagine. However, the process can be windy and tiring. However, walking the journey with my co-author, Prof. David Minja, makes the journey worth the while.

Our writing life would not have been possible without the support of many people whom I would like to acknowledge and thank.

We are grateful to our respective families and scattered friends for their sincere support, shared meals, advice, perspectives, and friendship and for wandering the meandering path of life with us.

We are grateful to the team at Vernon Press. Their work has transformed our manuscript into a book worth the reading that is in your hands.

Finally, we would like to thank our cherished readers. To write gives us immense satisfaction. To have it received by you, dear reader, is an unexpected gift that keeps us grounded at the moment when all writing is born.

Thank you from the bottom of our hearts.

About the Authors

KIRIMI BARINE

Dr Barine is a leadership advisor, author, and speaker with over two decades of engaging in leadership training and development in Africa and other parts of the world. His experience gained through various leadership positions with different organisations gives him the aptitude to equip, challenge, and inspire leaders across multiple spheres of influence.

Dr. Barine serves as the Global Publishing Development Consultant at the United Bible Societies, a membership organisation with over 150 member nations serving over 240 countries and regions worldwide. He previously served as the Publisher and chief executive at Evangel Publishing House. In addition, he is the founding director of the Publishing Institute of Africa.

Dr. Barine is an accomplished author. His recent works include co-editor for the African Christian Leadership: Realities, Opportunities, and Impact book, the result of a multiyear study implemented by African scholars, offering insights on the support and training necessary to promote African Christianity and to foster the healthy development of Africa (AfricaLeadershipStudy.org). In addition, he has edited, authored and co-authored several books, among them The Resilient Christian Leader: Experiences, Strategies & Opportunities in Times of Crisis, Every Leader's Battle: Experiences, Encouragement and Lessons from 10 Leaders, and Transformational Corporate Leadership, among others.

Dr. Barine enjoys training, coaching and building capacity for leaders, writers, and publishers and has been featured as a keynote speaker, workshop or breakout session facilitator at many conferences. He is a founding trustee for Media Associates International-Africa and a trainer with Media Associates International.

Dr. Barine holds a Doctor of Philosophy (PhD) in Business Administration. His research focus was on leadership and corporate governance.

DAVID MINJA

Professor David Minja is a Full Professor of Strategy, Governance and Public Policy at Kenyatta University, a researcher, an author, a leadership, governance and public policy consultant and a thinker whose writings and seminars have contributed to the philosophical and practical dimensions of strategic leadership, governance and public policy in Africa and beyond.

David is the Chairman of the Department of Public Policy and Administration at Kenyatta University. He has also been a visiting professor at universities across Europe and Africa. He has previously held Board positions in public and private sector organisations. He holds a doctorate in Organization Development from Cebu Doctors University in the Philippines, MA, Leadership from Pan Africa Christian University in conjunction with Trinity Western University-Canada and BA in Economics from Kenyatta University. He has co-authored several books and over 70 articles in internationally peer-reviewed journals.

List of Figures and Tables

Figures

Table

Section I:
Theory

1.

Introduction to Corporate Governance

The last two decades have seen the evolution of governance from a mere concept to a more fundamental discipline in social and economic circles. Avellaneda (2010), in a paper titled, "Good Governance, Institutions and Economic Development: Beyond the Conventional Wisdom," and presented at the *Forum de Recerca, Department de Ciencies Politiques I Socials, Universitat Pompeu Fabra*, Barcelona, observes that a growing literature stresses that governance, broadly defined as the traditions and institutions that determine how authority is exercised in a country, matters to economic development.

According to the Good Governance and Human Rights Organisation, there is no single and exhaustive definition of "good governance," nor is there a delimitation of its scope that commands universal acceptance ("Economic Rationality," 2009). The term is used with great flexibility; this is an advantage but also a source of some difficulty at the operational level. Depending on the context and the overriding objective sought, good governance has been said at various times to encompass: full respect of human rights, the rule of law, effective participation, multi-actor partnerships, political pluralism, transparent and accountable processes and institutions, an efficient and effective public sector, legitimacy, access to knowledge, information and education, political empowerment of people, equity, sustainability, and attitudes and values that foster responsibility, solidarity and tolerance (UN, n.d.)

WHAT IS CORPORATE GOVERNANCE?

Corporate governance is the system by which companies are directed and controlled (Cadbury et al., 1992).

Thus, governance is a system based on a set of practices to facilitate the development of enterprises that are accountable (McNamara, n.d.). Furthermore, governance includes the relationship between the exercise of power and the management of socio-economic resources for a welfare society. In the contemporary world of political pluralism, the concept of governance has become crucial and attracted great interest. Governance forms a significant component of the balance maintained between the quest for equity and order in society, effective production and distribution of goods and services, accountable exercise of legitimate power, respect for human freedoms and rights and finally, promotion of a socially and economically viable corporate environment that is accommodative to everyone's contribution (Monks & Minow, 1996).

The term "corporate governance" was first used in 1960 by Richard Eells in his attempt to define how corporate polity is structured and functions. However, the concept of corporate governance existed as early as the start of the 20th century, especially in finance textbooks. Moreover, the origins of this concept form the core basis of the definition of corporate governance. The constituents of corporate governance include processes, customs, policies, laws and regulations stipulating how enterprises should be administered or controlled. Equally important, corporate governance outlines the way stakeholders should relate and lays out corporate goals. Key corporate decision-makers include shareholders, management, and the board of directors. Stakeholders in the corporate governance structure consist of the workforce, suppliers, customers, financial institutions, and regulators, as well as the surrounding community.

According to Cadbury et al. (1992), corporate governance consists of the systematic control and direction of enterprises. Furthermore, corporate governance can be described as a set of management practices adopted by companies in the process of separating ownership and core business operations. The benefits of corporate governance are best experienced in the presence of core values of transparency, accountability, fairness, and responsibility. This is critical in reaffirming the confidence of investors, stakeholders, and the wider community. Corporate governance provides a plausible arena for different players to meet and relate while reflecting on the principal goals of the enterprise. Corporate governance is the way different participants relate in the process of charting the direction and performance of an enterprise (Blair, 1995).

Blair (1995) further states that corporate governance consists of a composite of legal, cultural, and institutional procedures that outline the functions of public corporations, who and how to control them, and finally, the risk-to-reward ratio in their operation. This further implies that corporate governance exists in an environment with an established legal, economic, and institutional framework that makes it possible for any enterprise to thrive and give value to shareholders while ensuring sustainable development that is human-centred and responsive to the expectations of stakeholders, the environment, and the wider society.

The figure below shows the relationship between owners and people who benefit from an organisation, its board, and management.

Figure 1.1. Effective Governance Relationships

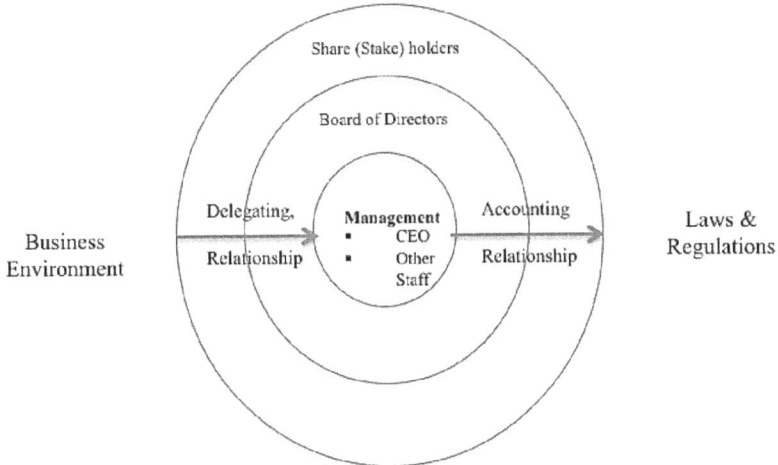

The Private Sector Initiative for Corporate Governance Trust (n.d.) in Kenya has undertaken to outline the principles of Corporate Governance as practised in Kenya. The initiative describes corporate governance as the procedure through which legitimate power is exercised in a corporation in the management of its aggregate portfolio of assets and resources to improve performance and profit maximization.

In broad terms, corporate governance refers to the way in which a corporation is directed, administered, and controlled. Corporate governance also concerns the relationships among the various internal and external stakeholders involved as well as the governance processes designed to help a corporation achieve its goals. Of prime importance are those mechanisms and controls that are designed to reduce or eliminate the principal-agent problem (Baker & Anderson, 2010).

The OECD provides the most authoritative functional definition of corporate governance.

> Corporate governance is the system by which business corporations are directed and controlled. The corporate governance structure specifies the distribution of rights and responsibilities among different participants in the corporation, such as the board, managers, shareholders and other stakeholders, and spells out the rules and procedures for making decisions on corporate affairs. By doing this, it also provides the structure through which the company objectives are set and the means of attaining those objectives and monitoring performance (OECD, 2005, p.3).

Various organisations have emerged to assist organisations in implementing sound and functional corporate governance principles. Examples include the Organisation for Economic Cooperation and Development (OECD) and the World Bank. In Eastern Europe, where they are especially active, they have been involved in assisting national governments as well as enterprises to improve accountability and, consequently, performance, and to adapt and carry out various codes of conduct and principles (Private Sector Initiative for Corporate Governance Trust, n.d.).

Corporate governance is the set of company tools, rules, relations, processes and systems designed for the fair and efficient management of the enterprise, meant as a compensation system among the potentially divergent interests of the minority shareholders, the controlling shareholders, and the directors of a company. Therefore, from the discussion above, it is clear that proper corporate governance is essential if an organisation is to survive and, more importantly, thrive. Corporate Governance contributes to the success of any institution and must therefore be prioritised.

EVOLUTION OF GOVERNANCE

According to Kanchinadham (2012), Kautilya's (also known as Chanakya) *Arthashastra* is the oldest book (around 300 B.C) on management available to the world. This book covered a wide range of topics and among its recommendations was that: The king should not consult with any advisor who has a vested interest in the outcome of a particular project. This is effectively the establishment of an ethical code of conduct - a subject that has received much attention, especially in the past few years of increasing corporate scandals (Kanchinadham, 2012).

According to Udo and Alexander (n.d.), until the beginning of the 17th century, partnership was the major, if not the only form for organising jointly owned business firms. Partners during this time took on unlimited personal liability for the contractual obligations of the firm.

One of the first corporations that came into existence was the British East India Company, sometimes referred to as the "John Company". It was a joint-stock company, which was granted an English Royal Charter by Queen Elizabeth I at the end of 1600, with the intention of favouring trade privileges in India. The company had 125 shareholders and a capital of £72,000. This was also one of the first companies established to gather investors to satisfy the huge capital demand of large projects and introduce a Court of Directors, thus separating ownership and control (Udo & Alexander, n.d.).

In *Transformational Corporate Leadership*, Barine and Minja (2011) provide the history of the corporation:

> The word "corporation" is derived from *corpus*, the Latin word for body, or a "body of people." In the late seventeenth century, Stewart Kyd, the author of the first treatise on corporate law in English, defined a corporation as, a collection of many individuals united into one body, under a special denomination, having perpetual succession under an artificial form, and vested, by policy of the law, with the capacity of acting, in several respects, as an individual, particularly of taking and granting property, of contracting obligations, and of suing and being sued, of enjoying privileges and immunities in common, and of exercising a variety of political rights, more or less extensive, according to the design of its institution, or the powers conferred upon it, either at the time of its creation, or at any subsequent period of its existence (p.35)

Entities, which carried on business and were the subjects of legal rights, were found in ancient Rome and the Mauryan Empire in ancient India. In mediaeval Europe, churches were incorporated in the same manner as local governments, such as the Pope and the City of London Corporation. The point was that the incorporation would survive longer than the lives of any particular member, existing in perpetuity. The alleged oldest commercial corporation in the world, the Stora Kopparberg mining community in Falun, Sweden, obtained a charter from King Magnus Eriksson in 1347. Many European nations-chartered corporations to lead colonial ventures, such as the Dutch East India Company or the Hudson's Bay Company, and these corporations played a large role in the history of corporate colonialism (Barine & Minja, 2011, p.17).

Adam Smith made this observation:

> Being managers of other people's money than their own, it cannot well be expected that one should watch over it with the same anxious vigilance with which the partners in a private co-partnership frequently watch over their own...Negligence and profusion, therefore, must always prevail more or less in the management of the affairs of a joint stock company (Forbes, 2007).

The industrial revolution brought about advancement in technology, which resulted in a wider diffusion of ownership of many large companies owing to the fact that no individual, family or group of managers could provide sufficient capital to sustain growth. Columbia University professors Adolf Berle and Gardiner Means, in their book, *The Modern Corporation and Private Property*, coined the phrase "the separation of ownership and control," which remains one of the most widely used expressions in the voluminous literature on corporate governance.

The table by Elijah Ezendu presented below lists international corporate governance initiatives which make up the International Corporate Governance Network founded by institutional investors in Europe and North America, the Global Corporate Governance Forum (2005) founded by OECD and World Bank and The Commonwealth Association for Corporate Governance founded by Commonwealth Heads of Government, among other initiatives (2010, para.12).

Table 1.1. International Initiatives on Corporate Governance

Year	Name of Committee/Body	Areas/Aspects Covered
1992	Sir Adrian Cadbury Committee, UK	Financial Aspects of Corporate Governance
1994	Mervyn E. King's Committee, South Africa	Corporate Governance
1995	Greenbury Committee, UK	Directors' Remuneration
1998	Hampel Committee, UK	Combine Code of Best Practices
1999	Blue Ribbon Committee, US	Improving the Effectiveness of Corporate Audit Committees
1999	OECD	Principles of Corporate Governance
1999	CACG	Principles for Corporate Governance in Commonwealth
2003	Derek Higgs Committee, UK	Review of Role of Effectiveness of Non-executive Directors
2003	ASX Corporate Governance Council, Australia	Principles of Good Corporate Governance and Best Practice Recommendations

Note: Adapted from "International Initiatives on Corporate Governance" by Rajkumar Adukia, Corporate Governance and Audit Committee as cited by Elijah Ezendu, 2010, para.12-13. Retrieved from www.slideshare.net/ezendu/overview-of-corporate-governance

WHY CORPORATE GOVERNANCE?

Good corporate governance is an essential part of the culture and business practices of any corporation. Monks & Minow (1996) observe that the government must explicitly adopt the policy that commercial competitiveness is a national priority and that an effective governance system is a necessary precondition. On their part, Bain and Band share the opinion that corporate governance is essential by pointing out that companies and other enterprises with a professional and positive attitude to governance are stronger and have a greater record of achievement.

According to the 2005 report by the Global Corporate Governance Forum, the many recent corporate governance scandals in America and many European countries have eroded confidence in the corporate sector. Salacuse, in a paper titled, "Corporate Governance in the UNECE Region," which was commissioned for the *Economic Survey of Europe* observed that financial scandals affecting major American firms, such as Enron, WorldCom, and Arthur Andersen, and the resulting loss of confidence by the investing public in the stock market have led to dramatic declines in share prices and substantial financial losses to millions of individual investors. Both the public and the experts have identified failed corporate governance as a principal cause of these scandals. The concept of corporate governance has evolved from just being a financial-economist terminology to being included in security trading by pensioners, employees and managing directors. The 1997-98 financial crisis experienced in Asia, Russia, and Latin America indicated that poor corporate governance practices were major contributors to crises leading to the downfall of entire economies. Moreover, the 2005 report indicated that poor corporate governance poses a great threat to the stability of the global economy and emphasised the need for improving governance in all economies in order to prevent economic disasters.

Equally important, policymakers have come to appreciate the greater good of sound corporate governance practices that go beyond preventing scandals and crises. Financial management is one of the greatest concerns and challenges of corporate governance. This is especially real in the contemporary world where firms are rapidly growing in size while at the same time financial intermediaries and institutional investors are increasing the scope of their operations. This has led to an increased need to differentiate the roles of owners and of management in the process of capital mobilisation. In addition, the process of allocating capital resources has been compounded by the opening and liberalisation of both the financial and real markets. Companies now have more risk exposure due to structural reforms such as price deregulation and heightened competition brought about by liberalisation. Consequently, the process of monitoring firms' capital management has become more complex, increasing the need for plausible corporate governance (Global Corporate Governance Forum, 2005).

Corporate governance has been necessitated by the negative amplification of indifferent attitudes displayed by oligopolistic, local power structures that provide accommodative grounds for selfish corporate insider dealing in the public and private sectors as well as other scandalous practices that leave a trail of havoc in countries' economies. The self-dealing by corporate actors leads to the mismanagement of crucial corporate-held resources and waste of capital to the detriment of the enterprise and the countries' economies at large, thereby propagating inequality and underdevelopment in developing and newly developed economies.

Good governance is imperative for the strong future of a performance-oriented enterprise. It provides an organisation with the competencies to align management practices with its vision and overall organisational goals and objectives (Governance and Management Ltd., 2005). Governance includes everything related to leadership. Therefore, a performance-focused board implements strategies that are able to improve the results of an enterprise, both in financial and social terms. Moreover, the board should be in a position to effectively employ funds and assets provided by the owner for maximum productivity.

A report by the Centre for International Private Enterprise (2002) titled, "Corporate Governance: The Intersection of Public and Private Reform," notes that just as good corporate governance contributes to the sustainable development prospects of countries, increased economic sustainability of nations and institutional reforms that come with it provide the necessary basis for improved governance in the public and private sector. Alternatively, corporate governance failures can undermine development efforts by misallocating much needed capital and resources and developmental fall-backs can reinforce weak governance in the private sector and undermine job and wealth creation (CIPE, 2009).

In an article by the Institute of Governance (2011) on why good governance matters, good governance is stated as a critical factor for the success of any endeavour, whether in the public or non-governmental sector. The presence of good governance practices clarifies authority, simplifies decision-making, and guarantees people and organisations are accountable for their actions and decisions. It further observes that studies indicate a direct relationship between good governance, stable governments and better social and economic outcomes such as higher per capita income, lower infant mortality, and higher literacy rates.

In addition to the broader positive consequences listed above, achieving good governance can have a tremendous impact on any organisation. Good governance according to the Institute of Governance (2011) promotes trust in the organisation and its people, improves morale among staff and stakeholders, enhances services to the public and stakeholders, improves decision-making and the quality of these decisions, connects the organisation and its board to its membership and stakeholders, enhances the perception of the organisation among people and stakeholders, improves its ability to weather a crisis and increases financial stability.

According to the Centre for International Private Enterprise (2002), the presence of strong governance standards provides better access to capital and aids economic growth. In addition, good corporate governance ensures that the business environment is fair and transparent and that companies can be held accountable for their actions. Conversely, weak corporate governance leads to waste, mismanagement, and corruption. They further observe that regardless of the type of venture, only good governance can deliver sustainable good business performance (CIPE, 2014).

According to the Centre for International Private Enterprise (2002), the main characteristics of success oriented corporate governance include risk management, performance improvement, increased access to capital markets, improved market environment, and leadership based on performance, transparency, and accountability.

THE ROLE OF GOVERNANCE

Masaoka & Alison (2004), observe that the board tends to have overall responsibility for a company's performance. It is also involved in support and team building activities as well as monitoring team and organisational performance. Notably, the board is a crucial team member in any organisation. The board is answerable to the owners/stakeholders in the corporate governance structure consisting of the workforce, suppliers, customers, financial institutions, and regulators as well as the surrounding community. Stakeholders in the corporate governance structure consist of the workforce, suppliers, customers, financial institutions, and regulators, as well as the surrounding community, employees, government agencies, and the community at large. The board should also be in a position to diffuse tensions that might arise within an organisation and between the enterprise and other market players. Furthermore, the board is responsible for designing practical strategies to strengthen the enterprise's independence as well as that of the governing authority. Evidence shows that boards must be ready to deal with a variety of situations within the span of their governance. For example, boards must govern during periods of crisis and are expected to be able to steer an organisation out of a bad situation. Therefore, the board should be able to leverage their expertise to overcome obstacles and uncertainties presented by any crisis (OECD, 2004, p. 17-24). Performance-driven boards go beyond their job description in times of crisis to ensure that the organisation remains solvent. They are involved in scrutinising financial statements, reviewing progress reports, and attending board retreats all in the effort to scale down the impact of a crisis. In the process of finding a solution to a particular problem, the board involves the assistance of various professionals such as financiers, legal experts, and business consultants. Equally important, in the event that serious concerns are raised against management regardless of the level, the board may consider hiring independent investigators or auditors to conduct an evaluation of the allegations and recommend any necessary actions allowed by law. Such allegations may include sexual harassment, corruption, mismanagement, abuse of power, or incompetence, to name a few. Crises demand that the board employ their governing expertise to see an organisation through this stage (Masaoka & Aliso, 2004).

It is not only in the time of crisis that the board's core competencies come into play but this should be the norm in day to day governing of an enterprise. There is a clear distinction between governance and management. The board is expected to respect the boundaries of management while adequately attending to its governance role. This does not in any way imply that the board should neglect its responsibility to question and monitor subordinate staff. In some instances, boards fail in governing their firms due to lack of time, lack of timely and relevant information, and simply not being in touch with the business. The board may also be unable to exercise its duty to dispel tension and conflict in an organisation. Moreover, the board may take a back seat in an event where the interests of executive staff will be compromised by a direct, hands-on approach. Similar to other desperate times, times of crisis in any enterprise require radical measures and as such it is quite common for tough questions to be asked. Moreover, the seamless running of an enterprise in stable conditions is rarely evident in a time of crisis. The board is under more pressure to exert its authority to chart the way out and forward. Governance involves setting very high standards for executive staff in the performance of their duties (Masaoka & Aliso, 2004). Additional areas of governance can be found in appendix 2.

CHAPTER SUMMARY

The study of corporate governance has gained momentum in the last two decades although old writings on the practice of good governance date back to 300 B.C. Many studies have been done in this field and many scholars have come up with different definitions of corporate governance. In spite of these many studies, scholars are yet to agree on a single definition of the concept of corporate governance although a number of them concur that corporate governance is the system by which companies are directed and controlled- a system based on a set of practices that facilitate accountability.

Good corporate governance is an essential part of the culture and business practices of any corporation because an effective governance system is a necessary precondition for strong and successful enterprises. In fact, corporate failure and scandals result from bad corporate governance practice.

Business leaders and policymakers have come to appreciate the greater good of sound corporate governance practices that go beyond preventing scandals and crises in organisations.

Financial management is one of the greatest concerns and challenges of corporate governance. This is especially real in the contemporary world where firms are rapidly growing in size while at the same time financial intermediaries and institutional investors are increasing the scope of their operations.

CHAPTER DISCUSSION QUESTIONS

1. Trace the evolution and growth of the field of corporate governance.

2. Why is the study of governance important?

3. What is the role of governance in organisational life?

2.

Governance Relationships

THE GOVERNANCE PARTNERSHIP (STAKEHOLDERS, DIRECTORS, COMPANIES)

Iskander and Chamlou (2000) present a dual perspective of corporate governance: that of corporations and of public policy. The corporation perspective, otherwise referred to as the private perspective, views corporate governance being about maximising value subject to meeting the corporation's financial and other legal and contractual obligations," while from the public policy perspective, also referred to as the public perspective, corporate governance "is about nurturing enterprises while ensuring accountability in the exercise of power and patronage by firms." The private perspective focuses on the need for board members to balance the interests of shareholders and other stakeholders–employees, customers, suppliers, investors, and communities – so that the long-term sustained value of the corporation can be realised. On the other hand, the public policy role is "to provide firms with the incentives and discipline to minimise the divergence between private and social returns and to protect the interests of stakeholders." From both perspectives, shareholder and stakeholder interests are at the fore of corporate governance (Geneen, 1984).

These two definitions—from public and private perspectives— according to Iskander and Chamlou (2000) provide a framework for corporate governance shown in the figure below that reflects an interplay between *internal incentives* (which define the relationship among the key players in the corporation) and *external forces* (notably policy, legal, regulatory, and market) that together govern the behaviour and performance of the firm.

The internal architecture defines the relationships among key players in the corporation while the external rules provide a level playing field and keep players in line.

In its narrowest sense, corporate governance can be viewed as a set of arrangements internal to the corporation that define the relationships between managers and shareholders. The shareholders may be public or private, concentrated or dispersed. These arrangements may be embedded in company law, securities law, listing requirements, and the like or negotiated among the key players in governing documents of the corporation, such as the corporate charter, by-laws, and shareholder agreements.

Figure 2.1. Effective Governance Relationships Internal and external factors that govern the behaviour and performance of a firm

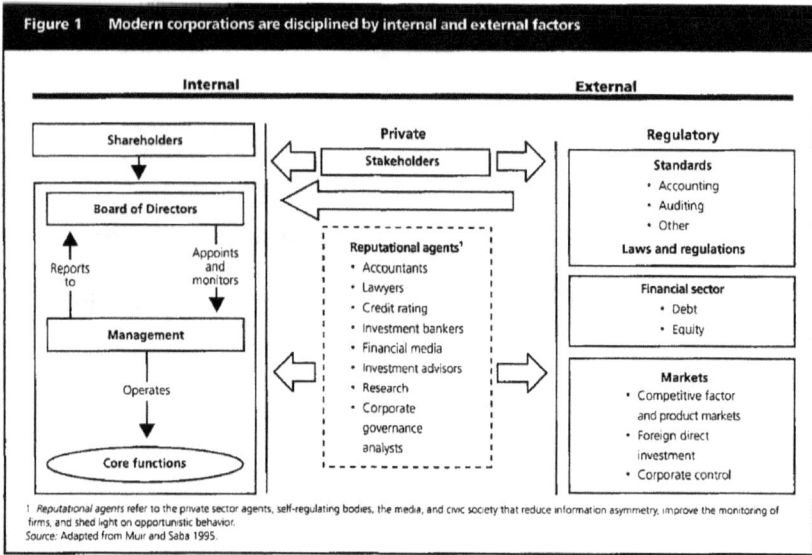

Figure 1   Modern corporations are disciplined by internal and external factors

At the centre of this system is the board of directors. Its overriding responsibility is to ensure the long-term viability of the firm and to provide oversight of management. In many countries, the board is responsible for approving the company's strategy and major decisions and for hiring, monitoring, and replacing management (OECD and World Bank report, n.d.).

Internal Corporate Governance

Internal corporate governance encompasses the controlling mechanisms between various actors **inside the firm**: the company's management, its board and the shareholders. In this form, the shareholders and other constituents "delegate" the controlling function to internal entities or mechanisms, such as the Supervisory Board (in case of a two-tier board) or the Board of Directors (one-tier) and/or special committees.

Examples of internal corporate governance mechanisms:

1. The Articles of Association and Memorandum of Association (the Corporate Charter of the firm)

2. Board of Directors

3. Supervisory Board (if a two-tier board) Roles: employer of management, supervising management, advising management), Structure, Remuneration)

4. Special Committees (Audit Committee, Compensation Committee, Nominating Committee, Governance Committee)

5. (Other) internal control procedures (Code of Conduct)

6. Executive compensation (is it fixed /variable, money/shares/options, based on short/long term targets)

7. The capital structure of the firm (is it equity or debt)

External Corporate Governance

External governance encompasses the influences from outside the firm on the governance of the firm. These can originate from a number of external sources.

Examples of external corporate governance mechanisms:

1. Markets

    •   Labour market (for executives and for employees)

    •   Product / services markets in which the firm operates, competition

    •   Capital market (debt, equity) (opinions of investment analysts, credit rating agencies, financial media, institutional investors)

    •   Market for corporate control (hedge funds)

2. Legal and Supervision

    •   National laws and regulations

    •   Supranational laws and regulations

    •   Corporate governance codes (e.g. OECD)

    •   Supervisory authorities (central banks)

3. Service Providers

    •   Independent auditors, external accountants (annual reports, financial statements)

    •   Investment banks (credit facilities, flotation, prospectus)

    •   Private equity

    •   M&A (takeovers)

4. Legal advice, insurance Media

    •   Public relations and communications (what media houses whether TV or newspaper report about your organisation, its employees and activities)

5. Relationship with unions (one such organisation in Kenya would be the Central Organisation of Trade Unions -COTU).

The OECD provides the following principles as a *starting point* for debate and consideration by governments seeking to raise standards of corporate governance:

a) *The rights of shareholders* (and other parties) to be given appropriate and timely information concerning an organisation, to take part in making decisions concerning essential changes, and share the profits that the organisation is making, among others. Corporate control markets should promote transparency and efficiency, and shareholders need to ensure that their voting rights align with the available costs and benefits. *Shareholders need to be treated equally,* especially in matters involving money and foreign shareholding. There needs to be full disclosure of information and the prohibition of abuse as well as insider trading. Board members and managers should disclose materials used in transactions according to the interests of shareholders.

b) *Stakeholders' role in corporate governance* needs to be recognized in accordance with the law. The corporate governance framework needs to promote active cooperation between the organisation and stakeholders. The end result should be the creation of wealth, jobs, and enterprises that are financially sound. There needs to be *timely and accurate disclosure* on all issues that relate to the company, including its performance, ownership, governance, and employees. Financial information needs auditing, and it needs to be done to high-quality standards.

c) *The board's responsibility:* the corporate governance framework needs to promote the organisation's strategic guidance, management's effective monitoring by the board, and the accountability of the board to the organisation and shareholders.

GOVERNANCE AND MANAGEMENT

Governance and management are two very core responsibilities that are fulfilled by a board either in singularity or collectively. Notably, a board's principal duty is to steer its enterprise, especially on governance issues. The board attends to this crucial responsibility with valuable assistance from the management staff. However, it is highly unlikely that any board will fully delegate governance responsibility to management. According to Mel (2006), governance consists of the accomplishment of targeted results and more importantly, achievement through appropriate efforts. Mel further observes that governance is about those decisions that have a positive impact on the organisation while promoting values in line with the vision, and it is the mandate of those in governance to establish plausible values, vision, mission, and overall goals for the enterprise.

Management consists of how tasks, people, resources, relationships, and technology are organised to achieve the overall organisational goal (Gill, 2005). The management team is mandated to steer operations in accordance with the pre-established framework and in line with organisational values and governance policies. Good governance practices clearly outline the difference in the responsibilities of the board and for management in an effort to pre-empt unnecessary overlap and conflict.

If organisational mismanagement does occur, the board is the one taken to task often with accusations of complacency. Unfortunately, most non-profit boards are not efficient in the way they govern. They further observe that weaknesses in governance policies may escape scrutiny until the severe impact of gross mismanagement is felt. The most prominent reason for such failure is attributable to discordant relationships between the board and support staff. This is in stark contrast with a team approach that the board, management, and support staff should adopt to achieve synergy towards the realisation of organisational goals. The team approach enables participants to use their different skills as well as play various roles in the quest to build the organisation. Often the role of the board expands beyond building and supporting to include questioning and monitoring the direction of the organisation in relation to its goals and objectives. The board should function as a team member and employ the necessary strategies to ensure that the organisation remains viable and competitive in a demanding market environment. Outside the team, the board resumes its governing role and must execute it autonomously and with the highest degree of accountability. In general, the board attends to the roles of support and governance, which include a variety of tasks. As support, the board's main objective is the success of the organisation. This is achieved through planned sourcing of funds, establishing networks, and providing and sourcing special skills such as accountants or legal experts, while representing the image in the community.

The Private Sector Corporate Governance Trust (n.d.), in their book, *The Principles for Corporate Governance in Kenya*, observes that governance is expected to be the protector of the interests of the public especially where an enterprise is more focused on profit maximisation (De Smet et al., 2007). In this regard, the governance mandate entrusted to boards includes sourcing and recruiting the top executive (for example the Chief Executive Officer) and subsequently carrying out routine performance assessments, reviewing and authorising plans, ensuring conformity with legal and contract requirements, and assessing organisational performance in relation to its goals. It should be noted that according to sound governance principles, the roles undertaken by the CEO, management, and the board, should be clearly distinguished. Equally important, good corporate governance engages in the promotion of effective and sustainable enterprises that benefit the entire society through wealth creation, employment opportunities, and solutions to existing as well as new challenges. Corporations with a culture of good governance are more responsive and accountable and they are more able to engage in legitimate operations. These kinds of corporations possess integrity, probity, and transparency as core values. Moreover, stakeholders' rights and interests are more secure and recognized in an environment where good corporate governance is the norm rather than an exception. In addition, corporate governance encourages an inclusive approach to running an enterprise emphasising democratic principles, legitimate representation, and stakeholder involvement. Governance supports processes, systems, practices, and procedures that facilitate plausible governorship of institutions. Furthermore, governance entails the application of formal and informal rules in governing enterprises and determines the preferred way of implementing such rules and other regulations and, as such, provides direction for dealing with relationships resulting from the rules.

THE FRAMEWORK FOR CORPORATE GOVERNANCE

The rules of corporate governance are based on both the laws and regulations in the legal framework of the country in which the company operates, and its own bylaws. Relations include those among the actors involved in the company: the owners (shareholders), the managers, the directors, the regulatory authorities, the employees, and the company in the wide sense. The processes and systems refer to mechanisms of delegation of powers, performance measuring, security, reporting, and accounting.

The Deloitte governance framework offers an end-to-end view of corporate governance and forms the basis for tools to help boards and executives quickly identify potential opportunities to improve effectiveness and efficiency (Deloitte, 2012, pp.2-3). Deloitte argues that the framework is not meant to be prescriptive but the concepts should be tailored to fit an organisation's specific circumstances. It should not be a replacement for existing models of internal governance but rather presents an integrated picture of the activities that comprise a company's governance system. The framework is not a tool for assessing legal or regulatory compliance (Deloitte, 2012, pp.2-3).

Underlying all the elements of the Deloitte governance framework is the corporate governance infrastructure. This is represented by the blue band that encircles the entire framework and is the aggregation of governance operating models —people, processes, and technologies — that executive management has put in place to govern the day-to-day activities of the company, as well as the processes used to accumulate information and report to the board and external stakeholders. According to the model, the board's role can vary from that of overseer to active participant with the level of the board's participation decreasing as you move from top to bottom. Deloitte's concept of risk and culture is at the core of the Framework and influences and impacts the effectiveness of all elements of governance.

For some elements (depicted in the bottom half of the Framework), the board's role could be thought of as that of active monitor, with the board understanding the operating models that are in place, determining that the models are adequately developed and resourced, and monitoring output and any issues identified in the process. There are four elements of the governance system that fall into this category for most companies — programs that provide control over the entity's planning, operations, reporting (both internal and external), compliance and risk management. The board's oversight objectives and activities within each of these elements are generally quite similar to one another, and may consist of understanding the company's operating models, considering their adequacy in the circumstances, and monitoring output. These same objectives and activities apply to the board's activities for the underlying infrastructure for each of the elements at the top of the Framework.

The top half of the Framework highlights areas of the governance system where the board's responsibility is typically greater. The board is an active party in the process either as a result of specific legal or regulatory requirements, or because of increased stakeholder expectations. Mere understanding and monitoring of the company's operating models in these areas is not sufficient. There are a number of specific duties and decisions related to each of these governance elements that cannot be delegated to company management. The board has a set of key objectives and activities for each of the governance elements, which include:

a) **Governance:** The board establishes structures and processes to fulfil responsibilities that take into account the perspectives of investors, regulators, and management, among others. The board selects its members and leader(s) via an inclusive, independent, and thoughtful process aligned with company strategy (Deloitte, 2012, p.5).

b) **Strategy:** The board advises management in the development of strategic priorities and plans that align with the organisation's mission and stakeholders' best interests, and that have an appropriate short-, mid-, and long-range focus. The board also actively monitors management's execution of approved strategic plans as well as the transparency and adequacy of internal and external communication of strategic plans (Deloitte, 2012, p.5).

c) **Performance:** The board reviews and approves company strategy, annual operating plans, and financial plans. It also monitors management execution against established budgets as well as alignment with the organisation's strategic objectives (Deloitte, 2012, p.5).

d) **Integrity:** The board sets the ethical tenor for the company, and actively participates in programs designed to promote legal and regulatory compliance and appropriate standards of honesty, integrity, and ethics throughout the organisation (Deloitte, 2012, p.5).

e) **Talent:** The board selects, evaluates, and compensates the CEO, and oversees the company's talent programs, particularly those related to executive leadership and potential successors to the CEO. The board communicates executive compensation and succession decisions in a clear manner (Deloitte, 2012, p.5).

f) **Risk governance:** The board understands and appropriately monitors the company's strategic, operational, financial, and compliance risk exposures, and collaborates with management in setting risk appetite, tolerances, and alignment with strategic priorities (Deloitte, 2012, p.5).

At the core of the Deloitte framework is risk and culture. When done properly, the oversight of risk and underlying corporate culture are not processes unto themselves. Risk Intelligence is at the centre of an effective framework for corporate governance - and it lays the foundation for everything the board and management do to govern properly. An organisation's success is, in large part, driven by how wisely it takes risks, and how effectively it manages the risks it faces, all of which take place in the context of the enterprise's pervasive culture. With boards taking a more active role in providing risk oversight, it's increasingly important for board members to have command of the issues that affect strategic decision-making and long-term success. The better everyone understands where the company is going and how it plans to get there, the better they will be at recognizing potential strategy killers (Deloitte, 2012, p.6).

The first priority of the board in the execution of its responsibilities in each board governance element is to understand inherent risks and the ways management is monitoring, assessing, and mitigating them (Zimmermann & Stevens, 2008). Most observers agree that the board has a clear responsibility to understand the risk management activities of executive management. This includes a detailed review of the resources devoted by the organisation, the quality and positioning of key risk personnel such as the chief risk officer, and the output of such processes. The board's role in risk oversight in some cases results in new or expanded regulatory requirements. Examples of these expanded requirements include the board's role in setting risk appetite and risk tolerances, understanding and monitoring critical risks (regardless of their origin), and providing robust disclosures about them to stakeholders. For instance, when considered in the context of governance elements, boards have a critical role to play in examining strategic risks, including risks to the strategy (which could cause it to fail) and risks of the strategy (which may result from successful implementation of strategic plans) (Deloitte, 2012, p.7).

According to the Deloitte framework, a board often frames its activities for risk oversight into two areas: oversight of enterprise risk programs (risk management), and oversight of critical risks and risk decisions (risk governance). Risk management is inexorably linked to the organisation's culture, characterised by the values of the entity, personnel motivations, and ways in which decisions are made. This Governance Framework was created to provide companies with a means for pinpointing the areas of its governance program that may need attention. The models are intended to provide a picture of effective governance to spark a board's thinking about the maturity of its program (Deloitte, 2012, p.7).

CHAPTER SUMMARY

This chapter begins presenting a dual perspective of corporate governance: that of corporations and of public policy. The corporation perspective, otherwise referred to as the private perspective, views corporate governance to be "about maximising value subject to meeting the corporation's financial and other legal and contractual obligations", while from the public policy perspective, also referred to as the public perspective, corporate governance "is about nurturing enterprises while ensuring accountability in the exercise of power and patronage by firms." The private perspective focuses on the need for board members to balance the interests of shareholders and other stakeholders – employees, customers, suppliers, investors, and communities – so that the long-term sustained value of the corporation can be realised. On the other hand, the public policy role is "to provide firms with the incentives and discipline to minimise the divergence between private and social returns and to protect the interests of stakeholders." From both perspectives, shareholder and stakeholder interests are at the fore of corporate governance.

Governance and management are also discussed in this chapter. The two are very core responsibilities that are fulfilled by a board either in singularity or collectively. A board's principal duty is to steer its enterprise, especially on governance issues. The board attends to this crucial responsibility with valuable assistance from the management staff. However, it is highly unlikely that any board will fully delegate governance responsibility to management. Finally, the chapter discusses the framework for effective corporate governance relationships. The rules of corporate governance are based on both the laws and regulations in the legal framework of the country in which the company operates and its own bylaws.

CHAPTER DISCUSSION QUESTIONS

1. Differentiate between internal and external corporate governance.

2. Discuss the frameworks for effective governance relationships.

3. Explain the relationship that exists between governance and management.

3.

Theories of Corporate Governance

According to Haslinda and Benedict (2009), it is highly probable that proposed models of corporate governance are flawed due to the conflicting personal interests of the social scientists developing them. This observation notwithstanding, Haslinda and Benedict (2009, pp.89-93) explore some of the fundamental theories that inform corporate governance including agency theory, stewardship theory, stakeholder theory, resource dependency theory, transaction-cost theory, political theory and ethics-oriented theories including business ethics, virtue-ethics, feminist-ethics, discourse, and postmodernism-ethics theories. These theories are discussed below.

Figure 3.1. Theories of Corporate Governance

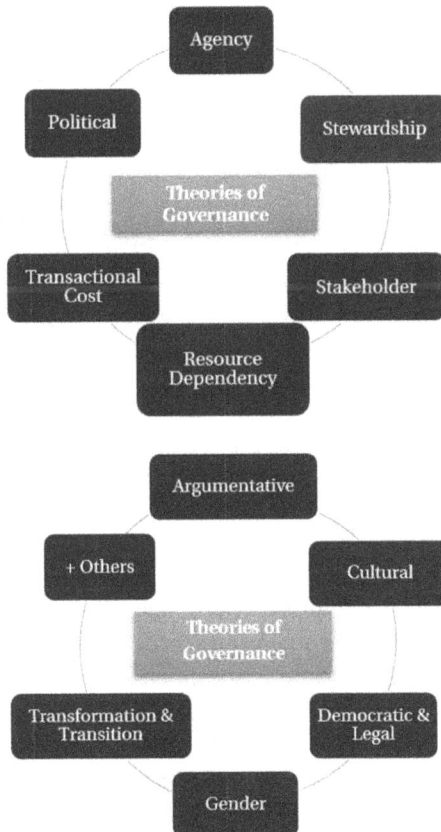

THE AGENCY THEORY

Agency Theory defines the connection between the principals, for example, the shareholders, and agents such as senior executives and management teams (Haslinda & Benedict, 2009). This theory designates shareholders as principals and outlines their capacity to hire the board and management as agents mandated to steer the growth of an enterprise. It recognizes the delegation of duties and responsibilities, especially from the principals to the agents such as directors and/or managers (Clarke, 2004). These two factors probably amplify the significance of the agency theory, and the theory's categorization of a corporation into two key players makes it conceptually simple to understand (Daly et al., 2003). Moreover, the agency theory implies the presence of self-interest on the side of the agents, namely, employees such as managers, in the process of discharging their organisational duties. Basically, the agency theory was prompted by the need to separate ownership and control (Bhimani, 2008). Therefore, it becomes very pragmatic when applied to evaluate the relationship between owners and the management structure. Moreover, agency theory encourages holding stakeholders accountable for the tasks and responsibilities delegated to them. This implies that employees are part of the governance structure and thus must contribute towards good governance as well as satisfying shareholder needs.

Figure 3.2. Agency theory

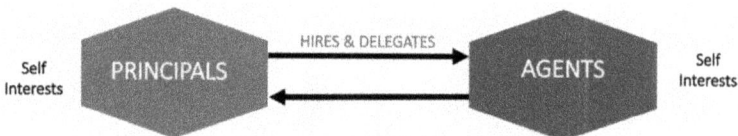

THE STEWARDSHIP THEORY

The **Stewardship Theory** was derived from psychology and sociology. According to Davis et al. (1997), a steward is responsible for protection and augmentation of shareholders' wealth through high productivity and performance. The steward is able to achieve this by maximising his/her utility functions in an enterprise. Stewards consist of executive officers and managers mandated by the shareholders to grow and protect their wealth (Donaldson & Davis, 1991). Furthermore, stewardship theory diverges from the individualism perspective of agency theory to a more elaborate perspective featuring the senior management team as the stewards whose career goals align well with those of the organisation. The stewardship theory assumes that stewards, notably, top management derive both satisfaction and motivation from the organisation's successful performance (Haslinda & Benedict, 2009).

Figure 3.3. Stewardship Theory

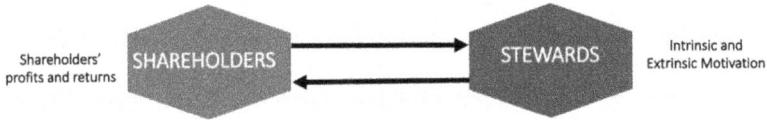

Note: From "Fundamental and Ethics Theories of Corporate Governance" by Haslinda Abdulla & Benedict Valentine, 2009, Middle Eastern Finance and Economics.

THE STAKEHOLDER THEORY

The **Stakeholder Theory** focuses on the group or person whose relationship with the organisation is a product of the organisational goals and objectives (Donaldson & Preston, 1995). Moreover, the theory helps evaluate the impact of organisational objectives on the people around it, otherwise referred to as stakeholders. The stakeholder theory identifies a network of relationships through which managers in an organisation serve. This is contrary to the agency theory that concludes that managers are the agents who work to serve the stakeholders and their interests. The relationships identified by the stakeholder theory involve management and suppliers, employees, and business partners. Furthermore, the theory is indicative of the importance of such relationships in comparison to that of the owner-manager-employee relationship identified in the agency theory (Freeman, 1999, p. 233). Equally important, the stakeholder theory attempts to prioritise the stakeholders' need for management's attention, (Donald & Preston, 1995). The theory outlines a seamless structure of relationships from managerial decision-making to addressing stakeholder interests, while exercising fairness and transparency in resource allocation.

Figure 3.4. The Stakeholder Theory

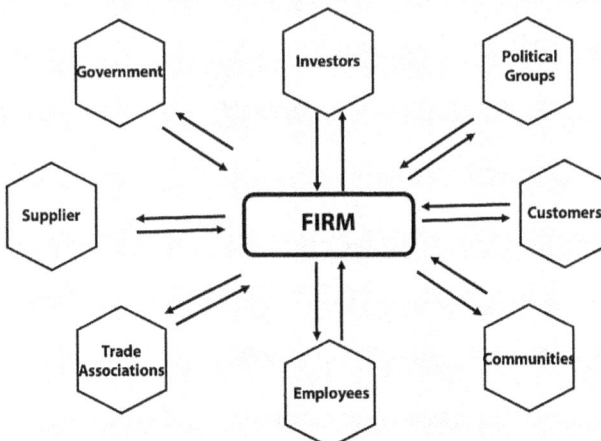

THE RESOURCE DEPENDENCY THEORY

The **Resource Dependency Theory** is a rationalisation of the board, its role in allocating resources to the firm, and its overall mandate. This theory plays a crucial part in demystifying the role a board plays for ensuring the availability and security of resources necessary for organisational functioning. This theory establishes that the board must develop external relationships to guarantee reliable access to the resources required by an enterprise (Hillman, Canella and Paetzold, 2000). Moreover, proponents of this theory argue that the appointment of representatives from autonomous organisations is a key determinant of the ease of accessing necessary resources crucial for successful performance. For example, having external directors who also double as partners in a law firm, translates to reduced costs for legal advice regardless of whether it is given within a board meeting setting or by private arrangement with the members. Moreover, directors from different professional and personal backgrounds bring an array of resources to the organisation, i.e., expertise, information, networks, links to suppliers, customers, policy makers as well as legitimacy (Williamson, 1996).

THE TRANSACTION COST THEORY

The **Transaction Cost Theory** was conceptualised and developed by Cyert and March in 1963. The theory was later refined and publicised by Williamson in 1996. Williamson described the theory as an interdisciplinary integration of law, economics, and organisation (1996). The transaction cost theory approaches the firm as an entity that accommodates people with varying views and objectives. The principal assumption of the theory indicates that organisations have grown enormously in size and influence to the extent of adopting the market's role of allocating resources. For example, the structure and organisation of an enterprise can provide it with a competitive edge for setting price and production benchmarks. The transaction cost theory uses transactions as the preferred unit of analysis. Williamson (1996) observed that managers, from the perspective of transaction-cost theorists, are opportunists and plan the firms' transactions with their interests at the fore.

THE POLITICAL THEORY

The **Political Theory** is a radical departure from the conventional tendencies of vote buying, to a more democratic and transparent system that demands vote support from shareholders. This theory indicates that promotion of corporate governance by political interests will have a significant impact on organisational governance. The government is the guardian of public interest in the process of corporate decision-making especially with respect to specific cultural experiences. Political theorists have developed a model that outlines various organisational activities such as allocation of corporate power, profits and privileges, taking into consideration the government's role. This model has the potential for influencing and facilitating development of corporate governance. In the contemporary world, national governments have increased their influence on matters of organisational governance primarily in their role of securing public interests. However, this has led to a tendency for negative political interference in the governance of a firm (Hawley & Williams, 1996).

The IK Vienna School of governance provides additional theories of governance. These theories are categorised as argumentative theories and address the causational forces that facilitate and precede the emergence and exercise of different governance practices as briefly outlined below (IK Vienna School of Governance, n.d., para 2-12).

ARGUMENTATIVE THEORIES

Argumentative Theories mainly put emphasis on language as a core component in any successful policy formulation process. These theories of governance tend to adopt a post-positivist epistemology based on social theory and methodology in the process of policy analysis. The process employs theoretical approaches including post-structuralism, discourse analysis, frame analysis, and interpretive policy analysis (Dean, 1999).

According to Fischer (2003), the epistemological orientation is helpful in understanding that institutions are established under their acts of description and use. This is contrary to the traditional mind-set that institutions of governance exist simply to be found by policy makers or the public benefiting from them (Fischer, 2003).

THE CULTURAL THEORY

The **Cultural Theory** was preceded by two historical transformations namely the "linguistic transformation" that occurred in the seventies, and the "cultural transformation". The latter happened a bit later and prompted refocusing and consequently, reforming the field of humanities. This was the inception of what is referred to as the second wave of qualitative approaches that gave great prominence to social sciences in the 1980s. Equally important is the fact that cultural theory is highly representative of modern politics. This includes capturing dynamic consumer and voter preferences, and letting go of traditional social relations and political affiliations in favour of a transformative society that is more tolerant to new cultural formation patterns and minimal political interference in governance (Gibbins, 1989; Gibbins & Reimer, 1999). The evolution of the cultural theory has contributed to a constant increase in application of culture both as a term and a concept especially in the description of political variables as well as experience in the mass media. Cultural theory has led to improved evaluation measures for understanding explanatory forces in the contemporary world of politics.

THE DEMOCRATIC AND LEGAL THEORY

The **Democratic and Legal Theory**: Improved understanding of democracy and how it impacts governance practices has been enhanced by the extension of political analysis especially by focusing on societal subcultures. This has been made possible through the use of cultural studies alongside redefinition of the term political culture with new information from both political science and anthropology. Participatory aspects of decision-making characterise the contemporary concept of democratic governance. (Huntington, 1991)

THE GENDER THEORY IN POLITICAL SCIENCE

The **Gender Theory in Political Science** focuses on the relationship between politics and policy frameworks and the existence of structural gender differences and inequalities (Thompson, Ellis & Wildavsky, 1990). Additionally, gender theory depicts the impact of structural gender regimes on political domains, policies, and politics. The theory employs gender integration practices as the variable in the understanding of political behaviour and thinking, gender inequalities and how genders relate (Scott, 1990). In the realm of political science, studies of gender-based issues mostly adopt institutional approaches based on democratic and state-oriented theories as well as consensus-building approaches in policymaking.

THEORIES OF TRANSFORMATION AND TRANSITION

Theories of Transformation and Transition: Transformation and transition theories are crucial in explaining a change process and the best way to handle it. In general terms, change may refer to transitions from one type of leadership to another, for example, from liberal capitalism to social welfare (Bleiklie & Kogan, 2000). This theory is also instrumental in highlighting potential obstacles that emerge for governance in the event of a change process.

CHAPTER SUMMARY

This chapter begins by arguing that it is highly probable that proposed models of corporate governance are flawed due to the conflicting personal interests of the social scientists developing them. This observation notwithstanding, some of the fundamental theories that inform corporate governance include agency theory, stewardship theory, stakeholder theory, resource dependency theory, transaction-cost theory, political theory and ethics-oriented theories including business ethics, virtue-ethics, feminist-ethics, discourse, and postmodernism-ethics theories.

Out of these several theories, agency, stewardship and stakeholder theories seem to be more prominent than the other theories among many scholars and practitioners. No one theory provides a comprehensive discourse of corporate governance theories, implying that these theories play a complementary role.

CHAPTER DISCUSSION QUESTIONS

1.   Discuss the various theories of corporate governance.

2.   Show how different theories address an important aspect of corporate governance practice.

4.

Models of Corporate Governance

Corporate governance models provide rules and appropriate control mechanisms through which shareholders can supervise the decisions of managers, and additionally, partners can be monitored and motivated. There is no one model of corporate governance, which is universally acceptable, as each model has its own advantages and disadvantages (Stahlke, 2003). The following are some of the models of corporate governance.

THE POLICY GOVERNANCE MODEL

The **Policy Governance Model** was developed by John Carver in order to prove that governance as a function is more closely related to ownership than operation (1997). The theory indicates that the role of the board is to add value to the interests of the shareholders rather than to be concerned with the welfare of managers. Therefore, the main responsibility of the board is inspired by the owner-representative accountability principle and the need to delegate more power to management (Drucker, 1974). Furthermore, Drucker (1974) concluded that most corporate boards share one thing: functionality failure. Moreover, in other literature, boards have been described as largely lacking in relevance, especially in the 21st century organisation (Gillies, 1992). In 20th-century texts, the board was branded with names such as pawns (Lorsch, 1989), ornaments, and detached from the daily operations of an organisation while still assuming they were in control (Leighton & Thain, 1997). The policy governance model proposes a set of principles as guidelines for good corporate governance. The model prescribes universally acceptable and applicable principles that qualify to be a model or a governance theory. However, to date, no single universally accepted and applicable theory of governance has been developed (Mueller, 1996). According to Leighton and Thain (1997), there is no universal description, theory, or model that is representative of the board system. Moreover, it would be virtually impossible to designate a specific definition of the board system to command universal acceptance. In contrast, Carver (1997) opposed this observation and prescribed the Policy Governance model as the answer to the missing link in the governance theory.

The policy governance model accommodates several assumptions. This includes the notion that the board represents the owner in reality. Therefore, the board can only exercise the authority derived from its roles in order to secure the interests of the shareholders. Hence, the board cannot delegate its prerogatives to the employees regardless of their management level (Gayle, 2003). The board also has the power to dominate over its subcomponent and ensure that they do not overtake its assumed prerogatives. This implies that any form of authority exercised within an organisation must come from the board in a legitimate structure of delegation. This designates the board as the supreme authority only second to the shareholders, and thus it must be in control of its responsibilities before extending its influence to other departments (Carver, 1997). The board as a group must be answerable for the actions of individual members, the entire group, and the delegations it commissions. At some point, it finds itself in a paradoxical dilemma: In order to fully cover its responsibilities to the satisfaction of all stakeholders, the board must dominate the chief executive officers. At the same time, productive and successful CEOs require some degree of autonomy from the board in order to exercise their given managerial powers effectively (Carver, 1997).

The policy governance model is instrumental in differentiating the main goals and the means of achieving them (Hogan, 2006). The policy governance paradigm divides the roles of the board and the powers they attribute to it and the adequate authority to be delegated to the chief executive. This is done through keeping corporate goals under check by way of elaborate affirmative policies and by controlling corporate processes in a proscriptive way (Carver, 1997). Corporate goals include the expectations of various classes of shareholders and their preferences. This means the purpose for which a corporation was established. The process describes what the corporation does rather than what it is (Argenti, 1993). For example, an organisation's principal business might be to grow shareholder investments through profit-making rather than developing an industry in the community. Moreover, corporate processes include all the decisions and realities that may not all make the list of main goals. Processes are characterised by activities, common practices, systems, technological advancements as well as a set of operational-decision fields. The board should inform any potential CEO of its performance expectations to avoid future misunderstandings during performance review. This is done in accordance with the policy governance model principle of affirmative and prescriptive control. Equally important, board expectations are to be based on projected returns, present market share price, and legitimately agreed-upon success benchmarks to be reviewed by the shareholders whom the board represents (Carver, 1997). This approach provides the board with ample time and resources to attend to its responsibilities and at the same time be accountable to shareholders, while giving management their space to perform.

The approach also empowers the management team at all levels. The board should always be in firm control of its meetings as well as external and internal relationships. This will ensure that management only supplies the board with relevant and accurate information to act upon. The board has various practical strategies to ensure it is firmly in control of the overall running of an organisation. The most notable strategy is based on the board identifying and clearly delineating its internal and external relationships and ensuring that it is not unduly influenced towards unexpected decisions. In addition, the board must stay together as a single unit in order to be able to maintain its authoritative rank of owner-representative (Carver, 1997).

THE ANGLO-AMERICAN MODEL

The **Anglo-American model** of corporate governance (specific for firms from the U.K., but also for those from the USA, Hong Kong, and Australia) tends to give significance to the shareholders' interests and emphasises radical innovation and cost competition (Laura, 2008). The model favours an outsider-based system while dealing in capital markets for activities such as new acquisitions and mergers of listed companies. Notably, all the countries that have adopted the Anglo-American model boast of strong and versatile capital markets and investor protection policies. Despite the geographical dispersion among the countries that employ the Anglo-American model, there is negligible variation between the versions implemented in these countries. The most common aspect of this model in all countries is the emphasis on, and respect for board independence and its supervision of management's activities for the overall achievement of the organisation (Laura, 2008).

THE CONTINENTAL EUROPEAN (GERMAN)

The **Continental European (German)** model is common in continental Europe as well as Japan. This model adopts an insider-based system and is not focused on the strong influence used by active capital markets, but on the existence of strong stakeholders, such as banks. Moreover, the model appreciates the value added to an organisation by employees, managers, suppliers, customers, and the wider community, and based on this premise it focuses on securing their interests. It is designed to promote innovation and competition (Laura, 2008).

This model derives its attributes primarily from the social and commercial context in practice. Thus, in Germany and Japan, the model facilitates the preservation of a culture where shareholders with high stock portfolios have a right to be actively involved in running an enterprise.

Their role is to sanction low quality management, to stimulate economic efficiency and to harmonise the interests of the firm's social partners, including its staff. Equally important, the Continental European model assigns a high degree of significance to human capital (Laura, 2008).

Whereas the Anglo-American model largely depends on the performance of the capital markets to determine its own performance, the European model depends on the stability and performance of financial systems, especially banks. Although in Germany and in Japan banks do not have high stocks as a part of the firms they finance, they exert a strong influence and control over their governance system. This model has received deserved applause for efficient monitoring and ease of access to finances by firms, and the establishment of effective communication structures between firms and financial institutions. The strong bank presence in management supports the firm's stability and commitment towards improved economic performance (Laura, 2008).

THE GOVERNANCE EXCELLENCE MODEL (GEM)

The Governance Excellence Model illustrates the keys for boards to do their part in making their organisations successful. Shown as a diamond—a GEM—it has seven facets or areas of responsibility described as core competency areas for a high-performing institution (Jim Brown, 2006). These seven disciplines are: Respect, Reflect, Select, Connect, Protect, Direct, and Expect.

1. **RESPECT owners' Expectations**

    - Invite input from the owners (the shareholders or members).

    - Help owners understand board actions and organizational results.

2. **REFLECT on organizational Results**

    - Understand and think about the results of the organization's operations.

    - Consider the reasons for deviations.

3. **SELECT Prominent Leadership**

    - Choose board members and officers with skills and values to project organizational credibility.

    - Remove people from these roles if they compromise the organization's effectiveness.

4. **CONNECT For Healthy Board Relations**

    - Agree upon, understand and comply with the expectations.

    - Capitalize on the strengths each brings to the team, insisting on full engagement. **DIRECT Organizational Performance**

    - Define and refine the vision, mission, and values.

    - Determine key result areas.

5. PROTECT The Interest of the Owners

- Create and use a monitoring system

6. EXPECT Great Board-Management Interaction

- Articulate board expectations of the organization and CEO and the evaluation process.

- Foster an effective team communication and teamwork between the board and the CEO

Figure 4.1. Governance Excellence Model (GEM)

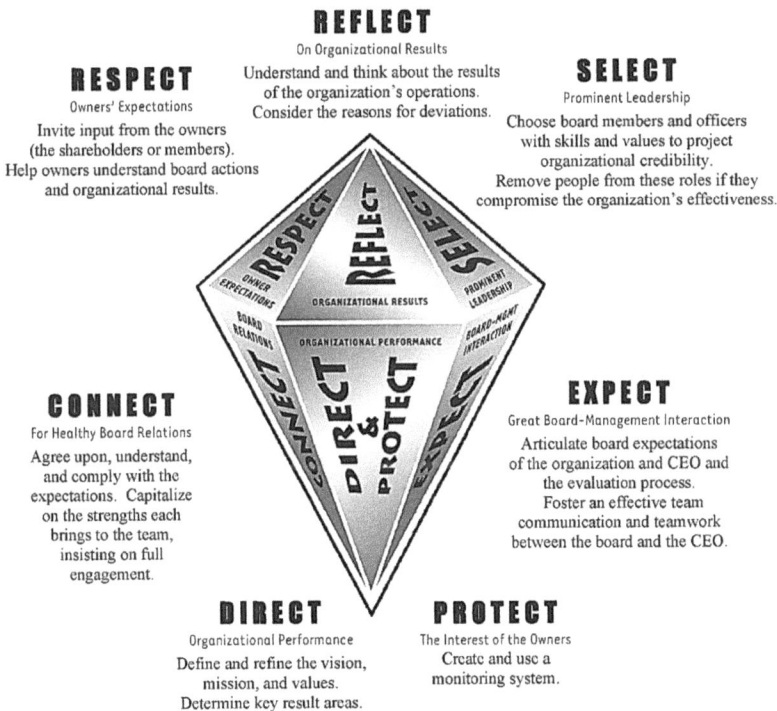

REFLECT
On Organizational Results
Understand and think about the results
of the organization's operations.
Consider the reasons for deviations.

RESPECT
Owners' Expectations
Invite input from the owners
(the shareholders or members).
Help owners understand board actions
and organizational results.

SELECT
Prominent Leadership
Choose board members and officers
with skills and values to project
organizational credibility.
Remove people from these roles if they
compromise the organization's effectiveness.

CONNECT
For Healthy Board Relations
Agree upon, understand,
and comply with the
expectations. Capitalize
on the strengths each
brings to the team,
insisting on full
engagement.

EXPECT
Great Board-Management Interaction
Articulate board expectations
of the organization and CEO and
the evaluation process.
Foster an effective team
communication and teamwork
between the board and the CEO.

DIRECT
Organizational Performance
Define and refine the vision,
mission, and values.
Determine key result areas.

PROTECT
The Interest of the Owners
Create and use a
monitoring system.

© 2008 GEM Governance Excellence Model

Note: "The Governance Excellence Model" reprinted from The Imperfect Board Member by Jim Brown, 2006, Jossey-Bass.

CHAPTER SUMMARY

Corporate governance models provide rules and appropriate control mechanisms through which shareholders can supervise the decisions of managers, and additionally partners can be monitored and motivated. There is no one model of corporate governance, which is universally acceptable as each model has its own advantages and disadvantages. Several models are discussed including, The Policy Governance Model, Anglo-American Model, The Continental European (German) Model and The Governance Excellence Model. Whereas the approach to governance differs from one model to the other, the emphasis by all the models is how to create effective boards capable of directing corporations and supervising management activities for corporate success.

CHAPTER DISCUSSION QUESTIONS

1.   Discuss the various models of corporate governance.
2.   Are there models that are superior to others? Defend your answer.

Section II:
Inside the Boardroom

5.

Board Fundamentals

A BRIEF HISTORY OF BOARDS

In the British colonies, as in Great Britain itself, the group of people who oversaw a company would meet regularly. Fine furniture was expensive in those days, and few people in trade had chairs or tables for the group. So the men sat on stools, around a long board placed across two sawhorses. The group was named "the board," after the makeshift table. The leader of the group did not sit on a stool and by reason of his prestigious perch was named the "chairman" (Monks & Minow, 2011, p. 255).

In the USA, boards continued the tradition that began with the joint stock companies, the earliest form of corporate organisation. The first commerce in America was conducted by two British enterprises that operated under royal charter: the Virginia Company of London and the Virginia Company of Plymouth. Two bodies governed these companies. The local council was a board of managers composed of colonists with the mandate of overseeing routine operations in the new land. It was accountable to another more powerful body in London, the "supervisory board," which was answerable to the sovereign and responsible for more general matters of policy and strategy (Monks & Minow, 2011).

Following the American Revolution, the new republic had to create its own form of governance. Alexander Hamilton was an early leader and one of the joint authors of the Federalist Papers and the nation's first Secretary of the Treasury. In November 1791, the New Jersey Legislature passed a bill authorising Hamilton's "Society for Establishing Useful Manufactures" (or SUM, as it was known). The society was allowed to produce goods ranging from sailcloth to women's shoes. The governance of Hamilton's corporation was surprisingly similar to that of today's largest companies. The Society's prospectus declared that a management board of thirteen directors would handle the matters of the company. Hamilton also created an early audit committee. He devised a committee of inspectors, separate from the board of directors, made up of five shareholders. They were generally chosen from among defeated directorship candidates, though shareholders could elect any five of their fellow stockholders. These inspectors were granted access to the company's books and given review power over all the company's affairs (Monks & Minow, 2004).

RELATIONSHIPS WITHIN A BOARD

The wide range of relationships established by the board conforms to a top-bottom structure including:

Shareholders: This group is the focus for the directors' attention, especially when the policy governance model is applied (Monks & Minow, 1996). However, there still exists some degree of disowning of the control structure by shareholders. When dealing with shareholders, the board is expected to avoid the use of the confusing and unspecified language of the corporation and rather implement plausible strategies to address shareholder concerns. Notably, shareholder interests rather than the organisation's stated mission and vision determine the board's duties and responsibilities (Monks & Minow, 1996). The term company or organisation usually refers to the management team and thus, in serving the company or organisation, the board might find itself deviating from its obligations to the shareholders.

The Board Chair: According to the policy governance model, the board is expected to take responsibility for governing a corporation as a single entity. However, this is not always easy despite the board members' competencies. The chair is a very crucial board member charged with ensuring that the board performs the group roles and duties to desired standards (Carver, 1999). The board chair is expected to ensure that the board remains accountable and does not encroach on the authority and duties of the chief executive officer.

The Chief Executive Officer (CEO): where good corporate governance is practised, it is important to clearly outline the board's relationship with and expectations for the CEO. In a structure of authority, the board emerges superior to the CEO and thus the board is responsible for supervising the CEO in a mutually accepted manner. Furthermore, the chair in an official, individual capacity has no authority over the CEO (Carver, 2000, para. 41).

Combined CEO-Chair: this entails merging the two roles. Consequently, this combination of roles compromises integrity in governance. Moreover, it brings about uncertainty in the direction and purpose of management affecting the performance of an entire organisation (Carver, 2000, para. 42).

Committees: are created by the board and thus remain under its rule and supervision. Moreover, keeping the position under the board's authority is a security guarantee for the board-CEO relationship and thus the superiority of the board (Carver, 1999). It is also vital for maintaining the wholesomeness of the board as a group. The sphere of influence of the committees is delegated by the board; for example, assisting the board in investigating a financial crisis. However, in the case that that sphere extends to advising and helping management, it becomes interference. Therefore, committees should always be restricted to the board's decision area that influenced their creation, i.e., audit, CEO remuneration, and shareholder concerns. Committees should never be created to steer human resources (Carver, 2000, para. 43).

Inside (executive) directors: this is a position in addition to being a board member. It is composed of a director who also doubles as an executive working for the CEO who is under the board's supervision. Apparently, this causes a lot of conflict in board-CEO relationship and performance (Carver, 2000, par. 44).

Lead director: this is an unofficial position identified by Ward (1997). The position emerges as a temporary solution to problems that emanate from a merged CEO-Chair position. In addition, the role of lead director comes as a complement to the board's autonomy needs and effective chairmanship (Ward, 1997). According to Mueller (1996), it is poor showmanship when corporate leadership refuses to let go of the traditional notion of the chairman or the CEO dominating the board. Mueller (1996) recommends a totally independent board and objective members not dominated by either inside directors, the CEO, or the chair. Corporate experience as well as a large volume of existing literature on corporate governance indicates that shareholders' goal of governance integrity requires a great deal of effort, time, resources, and focus (Carver, 2000, para. 45).

TYPES OF BOARDS

A board of directors determines the policy framework and strives to accomplish the organisation's mission and overall goals. The organisational bylaws (in the case of universities, the Charter documents and statutes) serve as guidelines for the board.

John Carver (2006, p 124-125) identifies four types of boards based on their position in the organisation:

1. **Governing board.** This is the topmost board that has ultimate accountability for the organisation. The authority of the governing board can only be exceeded by the owners or the state and they are also called corporate board, board of directors, board of trustees or board of regents.

2. **Advisory board**. The role of this board is to offer counsel rather than to govern. Advisory boards provide direction and guidance to the governing board, the CEO and other staff. The authority of the advisory board is limited to what is granted by the authority point.

3. **Line Board.** This type of board serves in place of a single manager. It is not advisory because it exerts some concrete authority over subordinate authority but is normally not at the helm of an organisation, and thus is not a governing board.

4. **Working Group Board.** This is a governing group with few or no subordinates or staff and thus the board both governs and works. The working group board is at the top of the organisation as well as everywhere else. The only way for this board to be effective is to keep the two roles clearly separated (Boarddevelopment, n.d.).

With regard to boards by the economic nature of an organisation, Carver (2006) identifies three types:

1. **Profit (equity or loosely termed business).** Governing boards in businesses can range from the statutory nominal board of a commercial business to a formal group representing diverse stakeholders' interests. For-profit corporations engage in business to produce a return on investment for shareholders.

2. **Not-for-profit boards.** Organisations that are registered for charity and have no stock ownership. These organisations are internationally referred to as non-governmental organisations (NGOs). In most cases, the legal obligations of not-for-profit boards are similar to those of other corporate boards.

3. **Governmental boards.** These are elected or appointed and are bound by more legal requirements in their composition as well as their processes. Governmental organisations are similar to not-for-profits with regard to profits and share of earnings.

Macnamara and Banff Executive Leadership, (2010) observed that there are many other models of governance written and being presented in governance circles today and that a different approach for looking at this issue is by Board type – which may have significant bearing on the incorporation of different components of governance into an effective model for each need:

- Ownership/Corporate Boards – with management or governance responsibility

- Advisory Boards – only need to give advice, no legal "governance status"

- Trustee/Pension Boards – only oversee assets, investments and/or disbursements

- Operational Boards – they do not have the financial resources that can hire full-time CEO or staff, and they have to do operational work and governance work for the organisation's sustenance.

- Marketing Boards – in charge of allocating quotas to different members who bring goods to the market, such as Chicken Marketing Board, Wheat Board, etc.

- Resource Board – oversee the environmental management of a region.

- Government Services Boards – the regional board that carries out the government's mandate at the federal or provincial level, such as Health Board, School Board, Social Service Board.

- Religious Board – "owns" some assets locally, and collaborates with faith bodies in doing so.

- Charity Board – fundraising and service delivery

- Professional Association Board – includes elements of self-regulation and professional practice advancement

a) Political: Town/Band Councils, Provincial/State Legislatures, Federal/Central Cabinets – often seen more in the light of the "politics" in which they engage and the policy agendas created; these bodies are equally responsible for discharging good governance for the mandated community (Macnamara & Banff Executive Leadership, Inc, n.d., p.5).

Gill (n.d.) puts across the necessity of a clear agreement between the executive director and the board concerning their relationships and roles for an effective governance partnership to take place. It is also essential to consider a group's size, its complexity, its geographical scope, and the agendas of the board members. All these influence the board's approach towards governance (Gill, n.d., p.3).

Furthermore, Gill (n.d.) notes that result-based approach is one of the emerging hybrid models towards governance, and it only requires a small number of committees around governance instead of management responsibilities. In almost all governance models that turn out to be successful, the governing body is in charge of coming up with a vision, securing resources, defining clear roles and responsibilities, setting standards for performance and keeping them in check, and being accountable to the stakeholders. All these require creativity in using practical knowledge as well as proper understanding of governance.

THE FOUR CRITICAL R'S FOR THE BOARDS OF DIRECTORS

The success of a governing body is dependent on the following critical "R's" that any board should take note of as summarised in the diagram below and discussed in detail thereafter.

Figure 5.1. The Four Critical R's for the Boards of Directors

1. Recruitment of Board Members

In the book *Transformational Corporate Leadership*, Barine and Minja (2011) discuss the recruitment of board members. The membership for advisory boards and boards of directors should reflect the diversity of the community, including representatives from various cultures, socioeconomic groups, and settings (rural, urban, etc.) as appropriate.

The following best practices are recommended for consideration in the recruitment of board members.

a) Recruitment ought to be in accordance with a well-developed plan. Both the board and the executive director must first start by reading the bylaws. They explain who is eligible to select new board members as well as the procedure that needs to be followed. The majority of organisations appoint a nominating committee to select new members. However, all board members and staff members need to be looking for candidates throughout the year.

b) Through the promotion of a recruitment campaign, the nominating committee must spot the skills required by the board, with the help of the board chair and executive director. The required skills might be specific to the service that the company provides (such as child development), or they may be general (such as accounting).

c) After the compilation of the desired skills and characteristics by the nominating committee, the current board of members can come in to collaborate in comparing the nomination list with the skills and characteristics. This will help in establishing the existing gaps on the current board, and it will help in narrowing down the search for candidates.

d) There should be a job description for the different board members so recruitment can be easier. It will ensure both staff and board members have an agreement on the role of the board in the company.

e) Potential board members may be sourced from consumers as well as civic business, and human service organisations. Others may be spotted from professional groups that are not represented in the current board (i.e., an accountant or early intervention specialist). Whereas it can help for influential community members to be part of the board, they must care about the organisation's services.

f) Potential members of the board should be contacted personally. A meeting between them and the board chair, a board member, or the executive committee can be held to discuss potential membership. They will need to be given materials to inform them more about the organisation before attending the meeting. These information materials will provide details of the organisation's professionalism.

g) When meeting with candidates, the company's representatives should discuss how each can contribute to the company. Such a meeting should have a job description to explain the role that one will be expected to undertake upon accepting the offer. It is essential to be specific when one is approaching potential board members. Doing this allows them to understand what they are being asked to do, which helps them know whether they should commit to the same or reject the offer.

After one's acceptance to serve on the board of directors or on the advisory board, it is essential for them to be oriented into the company. Board members should know how the company works so they can serve as they should. Giving them sufficient background information, a tour to the different available facilities and a meeting with the different key staff members can help them become more involved with ease. Also, giving new members concrete tasks will promote the ease with which they find a sense of belonging in the organisation. The board will also get an opportunity to offer new members formal recognition for their different tasks.

Individual board members will need to be trained on the issues of the organisation. This can happen through regular meetings or at meetings specifically held for training. Additionally, there can be annual board retreats to help in the integration of new members, building cohesion, and reflection on the company's performance for the past year. Training helps board members get involved and more educated about the organisation.

2. Roles of Board Members

Boards are created to provide leadership. Therefore, board members should possess dynamic skills and expertise for steering an entity in the required direction. This does not imply that there are no poorly performing boards. In fact, boards constantly complain about the lack of specificity in terms of roles and responsibilities. As they have rapidly evolved in the last three decades with a spiral effect on structure and responsibilities (Cyril, 1997), this has become more and more common.

Cyril (1997) defined the board in accordance with its three roles and responsibilities within an organisation:

a) **Governance:** The board designs and formulates policies that are strategic to the organisation's purpose.

b) **Management:** A tactical board is involved in the management and mobilisation of the human and financial resources necessary to accomplish overall organisational objectives.

c) **Operations:** These are the activities related to the delivery of the organisation's services or programs. The board has no mandatory role in this area (Giorgi, 2003). Many boards see this work as the responsibility of the staff. However, depending on their board model, some boards choose to actively participate in operations due to philosophy or limited resources.

Different boards have different mandates with regard to their organisational purpose and access to resources. According to Gill (2005), each board performs a distinctive set of duties and responsibilities including:

a. **Deliberate, design, establish, and routinely review an organisation's vision, mission, and purpose**. This responsibility includes keeping strategic organisational objectives up-to-date to reflect the needs of a changing global environment, conducting regular performance reviews for lower management, strategic management and overall organisational performance, and offering strategic leadership that guarantees the organisation's survival into the future.

b. **Oversee the organisation's financial stability**. This involves intensive resource mobilisation to secure adequate finances for organisational operations, designing and deliberating on annual budgets, implementing cost reduction strategies and ensuring transparent, responsible record keeping.

c. **Oversee sourcing of human capital** by routine review and improvement of the working environment, recruitment of the CEO, active participation in human resource policy formulation as well as establishing and ensuring independence for the board recruitment committee.

d. **Supervise organisational operations** to ensure that the organisation is compliant with necessary and relevant legal requirements, maintains board autonomy, improves its performance and sustainability, has regular assessments of organisational performance of its core activities, and provides maintenance, review, and updating of the organisational structure and risk management policy.

e. **Ensure the existence of cordial relations between the organisation, community, and other stakeholders**. This is done by developing a timely and functional response mechanism for dynamic environments such as technology and demographics, devising new technologies to address current and future challenges, implementing strategies that improve the firm's public relations portfolio and guaranteeing accountability and transparency to shareholders and stakeholders and thus keeping them confident about organisational performance.

In line with the high expectations placed on the board, individual board members have crucial roles to play to ensure that the board as a group steers the organisation in the right direction. Members of the board should have full knowledge and understanding of the institution's mission and vision as well as the extent of their mandate. Board members should always be furnished with relevant information. Members should be informed and have the power to question the organisation's financial and/or budgetary processes. In addition, board members should ensure organisational compliance with legal requirements and also protect the confidentiality of board deliberations and operations. Furthermore, board members should facilitate the implementation of a training program for career development within the organisation.

From a legal standpoint, trustees, officers, or members of a not-for-profit board are held to the following three standards as described by BoardSource:

1. **Duty of care**. Board members must be active in decision-making and represent the best interests of the organisation and shareholders (BoardSource, 2011).

2. **Duty of loyalty.** When acting on behalf of the organisation in a decision-making capacity, board members must set aside their personal and professional interests. The organisation's needs come first.

3. **Duty of obedience**. Board members bear legal responsibility for ensuring that the organisation remains true to its mission and purpose in compliance with all applicable laws. Not-for-profit boards vary in many ways including structure, leadership, workforce, performance and internal and external relationships and although all boards exhibit similarities in basic duties, they are also very diverse in their functions (BoardSource, 2005).

The Core Roles of a Board

In the not-for-profit sector of the economy, good governance is synonymous with efficient governance by the board. Members of the board are assigned the task of timely delivery of planned outcomes using appropriate channels. All boards share a common role of steering their organisation to high productivity and performance (American Society for Training and Development, 2005). Despite the variation in the board models, there is commonality in the job descriptions of most boards. This is better captured through the following three broad categories of governance roles presented in the table below.

Table 5.1. Core Board Roles

Roles	Functions
Representation	1. Represent stakeholders 2. Carry public trust 3. Facilitate board renewal via selection of new directors
Decision making and leadership	1. Establish or affirm mission: Development and/or custodianship of organisational purpose, mandate and identity 2. Strategic Direction: Provide vision for future; Develop and implement long-term plan; Set or approve general direction and financing; Ensure that mission remains responsive to changes in the environment and organisational realities 3. Provide an accountability structure for management; direct and advise management; select, support, evaluate and, if necessary, terminate senior manager 4. Financial Stewardship: Trusteeship of financial resources to ensure that funds are expended for intended purposes 5. Human Resource Stewardship: HR Policy Framework 6. Risk Management 7. Managing transitional phases and critical events: act as organisational safety net 8. Represent organisation to community
Accountability	1. Ensure transparency 2. Monitor and evaluate performance 3. Responsibility and reporting to stakeholders 4. Act as ultimate source of accountability under the law for organisational performance and actions

Note: Adapted from "Core Roles of the Board" by Mel Gill, Governing for Results: A Director's Guide to Good Governance, 2005, Victoria, BC: Trafford Publishing.

Duties of the Board (Best Practices)

The duties of the board can be summarised to comprise of the following:

(a) Formulation of policies and overseeing the Management and conduct of the business;

(b) Formulation and management of risk management framework;

(c) Succession planning and the appointment, training, remuneration and replacement of board members and senior management;

(d) Overseeing the effectiveness and adequacy of internal control systems;

(e) Overseeing the maintenance of the company's communication and information dissemination policy;

(f) Performance appraisal and compensation of board members and senior executives;

(g) Ensuring effective communication with shareholders;

(h) Ensuring the integrity of financial reports;

(i) Ensuring that ethical standards are maintained; and

(j) Ensuring compliance with the laws of the land.

3. Board Relations

THE BOARD CHAIR'S ROLE

James Verdonik and Kirby Happer (n.d.) provide the following roles of the chairman of a board of directors, which they say vary depending on a number of factors. The Chairman might be a CEO as well, or the president, or even all three, Chairman, President, and CEO.

A company's bylaws explain the rights and duties of the chairman. Generally, one is elected by the Board of Directors and they preside at the different meetings with board members and shareholders. They also frequently serve as company officers. At times, they serve as ex officio committee members.

When a chairman has no other role, such as CEO or president, their primary role becomes leading meetings of the Board of Directors. A company's size determines the chairman's leadership role. The role of leadership from the chairman is crucial when there are many board members and multiple interest groups.

It is advisable for an organisation to adopt procedure rules for meetings of Board, shareholders and committees, since the chairman may be called upon to make procedural decisions that influence the essential issues. Whereas procedure rules might not need to be followed to the letter, it is essential to establish a procedure that helps in dispute resolution, so the chairman can be objective and fair in their ruling. According to Verdonik and Happer (n.d.), the procedure promotes the essence in proportion to the conflict level in the company. Hence, it is essential for the chairman to be organised and follow the required rules and regulations as they have been put in place by state laws and organisation's bylaws, as well as other agreements. This ensures that there is effectiveness in the different meetings. When a chairman fails to go through the necessary steps, it is easy for their action to be challenged at a later time and get invalidated.

A chairman also has the duty to call meetings of the Board of Directors and shareholders. If the board is divided, the chairman has the power to call a special meeting and give the general direction that the company should take. The meeting can be called upon even when it has not been scheduled. Often, chairmen set the agenda for board meetings and this helps in giving the meetings their direction and scope.

What makes an effective Chairman?

Verdonik and Happer (n.d.) are of the opinion that a chairman must gain the trust of the Board of Directors and the company's managers and shareholders if they are to be effective as leaders and mediators. To gain the trust of peer Board members and management, the chairman must be fair.

A good chairman needs to be **open-minded**, and they should encourage board members to speak out their views. This is of utmost importance because of the belief that the best decisions are made when people freely share their views. When the chairman runs activities in a manner to discourage discussions, questions, and conflicting opinions, the effectiveness of the Board of Directors ends up being severely limited.

The chairman needs to make sure that **meetings are run efficiently.** Often, board members do not have sufficient time to attend all meetings, and they easily get bored or impatient when there are endless debates. To promote competition, business decisions need to be made quickly.

The chairman needs to balance between an encouraging discussion and the questions being presented for the meeting to move forward and for important decisions to be made within the required time. At times, the chairman will need to call an end to discussion, or require individuals to vote even though not all directors will feel they have sufficient time to persuade others concerning their views. Verdonik and Happer (n.d.) conclude is the hallmark of a good Chairman. A sample job description for a chairman's position is provided in Appendix 3.

The Executive Chairman of Rita's Italian Ice (an ice cream company in the US) Mike Lorelli gives his summary on what he believes a Board chair should take a lead on and what a CEO's lead should be.

The executive chairman or board chair takes the lead in running the board of directors, dealing with external funding (investors and lenders), joint venture pursuits and relations, compensation practices, management development, CEO succession and strategic plan guidance.

The CEO takes the lead in running the company, across its strategic, operating and organisational processes.

BOARDS AND CEO RELATIONSHIP

According to Lauren Murden (2012) in the article "The Board and the CEO Relationship," role clarity is essential to ensuring a productive CEO/Board relationship is founded. The following four key areas of defined responsibility are crucial to the CEO/Board relationship: Accountability, Decision-making, Policies and Financial Reports.

a) **Accountability**: Generally, the board has a role of accountability, which is to ensure that the organisation serves the needs of its stakeholders. It also needs to ensure it aligns with the compliance requirements. Directors need to act bona fide (in good faith) in the interests of the company as they are accountable to act in the best interest of stakeholders.

As the CEO is accountable to the board, he needs to ensure that he reports to the board and keeps it informed with regard to the activities taking place in the company. The CEO needs to balance the details that need to be given out in the different reports. However, the relationship between the CEO and the board should not be represented by frequent and onerous requirements for reporting. Else, the CEO will be diverted from their needs to build relationships with other parties, which is necessary for the organisation. Hence, performing responsibilities needs to be in harmony with the role assigned to others, and it should allow consistent communication and cooperation to meet the accountability requirements (Lauren Murden, 2012).

b) **Decision-making**: There are defined decision-making roles in the relationship between the CEO and the board. The board determines the organisation's decisions and is responsible for ensuring that goals are set and policies and corporate strategies are designed so that they address a company's mission and enable it to have measurable goals and objectives. Also, the bard puts in place discretionary financial and other relevant operating limits for the management. It also assesses the activities of the organisation and compares them to the mission to determine whether it is meeting its original purposes.

According to Lauren (2012), the decision-making responsibilities need delegation. Also, the board needs to reserve all matters that can possibly impact the company's reputation and financial stability.

The role of the CEO that involves the making of decisions is different. He is responsible for direction, goal, and policy implementation after they have been created by the Board. He also gets to report the operational outcomes. Furthermore, the CEO also gets to ensure that each individual in the organisation gets to know more about the agreed strategic direction, the organisation's goals, and the policies. In essence, he gets individuals to head in the same direction. The decision-making process by the CEO relates to the way that is best for the implementation of measurable objectives and goals developed by the Board.

c) **Policies**: Whereas the board is responsible for coming up with the company's policies, the CEO is in a better position to provide policy suggestions because he has daily contact with the different operators in the organisation. After all, it is the responsibility of the CEO to implement and monitor the company's policies. An effective relationship between the CEO and the board helps to achieve the policy goals (Lauren Murden, 2012).

d) **Financial Reports**: The CEO needs to present annual reports on the company's finances for the board to review and approve. Also, he gets to offer ideas and strategies that help the company to perform better. The board takes the role of reviewing, analysing, and monitoring the information that the CEO presents to them. Also, the board asks relevant questions to get the required information. Since the board is tasked with ensuring the organisation is financially healthy, it needs the CEO to cooperate and provide the information required to promote this (Lauren Murden, 2012).

Factors that may affect the CEO/Board relationship

According to Lauren (2012), some organisations have complex and tense relationships between the CEO and the Board. However, maintaining a healthy and professional relationship is necessary for the running of the organisation. At times, board members can feel excluded or disempowered, and they can struggle to secure the information they need from a CEO. In the same manner, many CEOs look at the board as though it were a monkey on their back because it keeps on monitoring and controlling their role in the organisation. The different factors that enhance the relationship between the two include the following:

a) **Respect**: it must go both ways in the CEO/Board relationship.

b) **Support**: it is a recognition that both parties are on the same side and working together towards a common purpose. Lauren (2012) indicates that ambivalence, whether existing or perceived, reduces an organisation's ability to function as it should, and this makes it difficult for the organisation to respond to change.

c) **Competence and consistency**: it does not only mean the applicable expertise that the individual directors of the board have but also the professionalism that enables them to conduct themselves as board members. It is necessary for the CEO to see consistency and certainty in the process of making decisions whenever they look at the Board. When a CEO loses confidence in the ability of the Board to support their proposal, they will not be confident concerning their position as CEO in the organisation.

d) **Clear communication**: it is essential for the board to get clear communication from the CEO, especially on matters that relate to finances and the administration. The information needs to be effectively presented, and the response to it should be prompt.

Mutual Obligations

Despite an organisation's type and size, the relationship between the CEO and the Board needs to be represented by "the best principles of teamwork – mutual respect, an understanding of one's own contribution, an awareness and reasonable degree of tolerance of each other's weaknesses and constraints and, overall, a sense of common purpose" (Lauren Murden, 2012).

According to law, the board is responsible for the organisation's accountability and authority. However, in practice, the CEO bears more power and authority. There is a need for both roles to be recognized as important roles for the company to run smoothly. Hence, a successful CEO/Board relationship requires responsibilities to be shared rather than having the attitude of "your job" "our job." There needs to be clear communication, coordination, and mutual obligation for the relationship to succeed.

Lauren provides the following as some of the Board's obligations to the CEO and vice versa:

Board's obligations to the CEO

- Compensation, benefits, and a working atmosphere that make the CEO's position attractive to the best possible candidates;
- A clear duty statement and performance goals;
- Regular formal performance reviews;
- Constructive informal feedback on job performance;
- Rewards for tasks well done; and
- Prompt and thoughtful response to requests for guidance or assistance.

CEO's obligations to the Board

- Commitment to company's mission and increased sensitivity to the communities being served;
- Responsible performance of essential tasks, both organisational and administrative;
- An administrative structure and decision-making mechanism that promote a productive working atmosphere and effective staff relations;
- Thorough and timely communication with the Board on financial and administrative matters;
- Effective representation of the organisation in the community and commitment to enhancing its public image; and

- Prompt and thoughtful response to Board members' requests for information.

4. Renewal and Board Performance

The Board should be of a sufficient size relative to the scale and complexity of the company's operations and be composed in such a way as to ensure diversity of experience without compromising independence, compatibility, integrity and availability of members to attend meetings and deliberate on issues affecting the business of the company.

THE EFFECTIVE BOARD

The enablers of an effective governing body are the processes, which provide the foundations for good governance; that is, they are the building blocks on which governance rests.

Figure 5.2. Enablers of effective governance

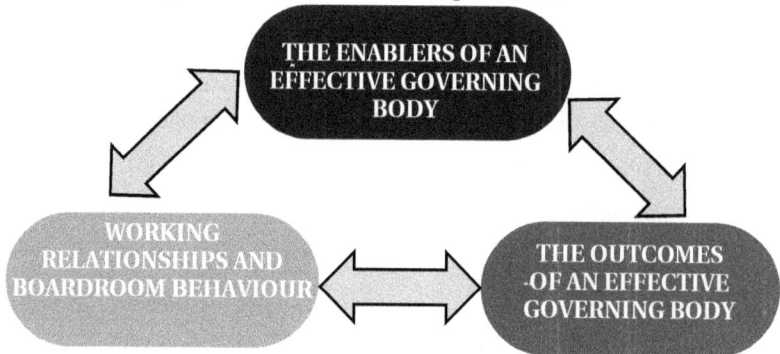

THE ENABLERS OF AN EFFECTIVE GOVERNING BODY

WORKING RELATIONSHIPS AND BOARDROOM BEHAVIOUR

THE OUTCOMES OF AN EFFECTIVE GOVERNING BODY

The Leadership Foundation for Higher Education, LFHE, (2010) has identified six factors, which are crucial to enabling effective governance. These do not by themselves lead to effective outcomes or added value from a governing body, but without them it is unlikely that effective outcomes can be achieved. In other words, these six enablers provide the potential for governing bodies to be effective.

1. Effective leadership and governing body dynamics
2. Effective governance structures and processes
3. Effective governing body membership
4. Commitment to vision, organisational culture, and values
5. Effective performance monitoring and measurement
6. Effective information and communication

Research done by the Marshall School of Business Centre for Effective Organisations indicates that to do their jobs effectively, a Board of Directors needs *knowledge, information, power, motivation,* and *time* (Jay Conger, David Finegold and Edward Lawler III, 1998).

1) *Knowledge:* The knowledge and experience of board members needs to match the demands that the organisation is facing. The board members' skills and backgrounds should be diverse and also complement each other. When directors are selected only from a single area of expertise, the board members end up only focusing on individuals' interests.

2) *Information:* A board needs much information about the organisation if it is to be effective. For example, it needs updated information on competition, key strategic issues, and possible acquisition targets. Also, the presentation of this information matters, and it needs to be presented concisely. The board needs to get this information from many sources, including outside stakeholders, employees, and the directors themselves. Therefore, when evaluating board resources, it is necessary to also consider the origins of the information being presented.

3) *Power:* For the board to be effective, it needs authority – the authority to act as a body that governs the organisation and makes essential decisions. One of the ways of ensuring that the board is independent in overseeing the actions of the CEO is by ensuring that the CEO is not the chair of the board. Even when one person takes both roles of being the CEO and the chair of the board, an organisation can still take steps that enable it to balance power between the board and the chief executive. One of the ways this can be done is by having a lead director acting as a representative of the outside directors when coming up with agendas for meetings. Also, this director would be in charge in times of crises. To maintain balance, it is also necessary to institute the formal evaluation of the CEO's performance and make their compensation dependent on their ability to attain targets that have been put in place by the board.

4) *Motivation:* It is necessary to put in place accurate incentives that align the interests of the directors with those that the motivation represents, including shareholders and other stakeholders in the company such as employees, customers, and the community. Certain actions by the organisation act as levers that the company can use to promote motivation among board members. Examples of this include the process of selecting directors and the reward system. The board evaluation needs to ensure that it identifies the requirements for

owning stock instead of cash, and it needs to analyse the mix of short-term and long-term rewards.

5) *Time:* To make the right decisions, it is necessary for the directors to spend time together as a group. After doing so, they should evaluate these meetings to determine whether they are having adequate meetings and whether there is sufficient time for them to address the issues that they need to address within the different meetings. For example, meetings should not be used by board members to get information that they would otherwise get from management if they communicated earlier. Instead, meetings should be spent to engage in substantial discussions and decision making.

WHAT MAKES A BOARD INEFFECTIVE?

Some of the issues identified by Shattock (2006) as reasons why a board is considered ineffective include the following:

- Unsuitable processes or structures, which will undermine governance.
- Board membership which is inappropriate for the defined roles and responsibilities, or where the skills and experience of board members are not used effectively.
- A lack of clarity in board responsibilities.
- An unduly dominant chief executive or senior management team, particularly one with little sympathy for effective governance.
- Inadequate information flow to the board and lack of a systematic approach for providing board information.
- Boards which lack coherence and whose members are acting as individuals with little identification with the best interests of the organisation as a whole.

In addition, Shattock (2006) indicates other less evident reasons for ineffectiveness:

- Weak board leadership by its chair and senior members - particularly debilitating if combined with the existence of a dominant CEO.
- A lack of motivation, willingness or time on the part of board members to address difficult issues or to challenge an executive constructively.
- A tendency to "group think" where dominant or conventional assumptions may not be challenged.
- An absence of trust and integrity within a board.

Based on the results of her study, Kezar (2006) identified six elements of effective or high-performing boards:

- Providing leadership through developing a common vision.

- Developing a culture and associated values, which guide board workings.

- Education, which refers to the support and development of the board.

- Ensuring effective external relationships: Here the study found that boards with large numbers of externally appointed or elected members (some with political affiliations) were likely to be different from those where appointment remained within the control of the institution.

- Building relationships among all stakeholders.

- Appropriate governance structures, of which five issues are highlighted: clarity of role; an effective committee system; careful selection of the board chair; on-going board evaluation; and the need for a board to act "as a collective unit."

PRINCIPLES OF GOVERNANCE OBSERVED IN EXCEPTIONAL BOARDS

Twelve core principles have been identified which empower some of the most exceptional and successful boards. According to the Board Source (2005) as cited by Dale Drummond (2006), the twelve principles of exceptional boards are:

1. *Constructive partnership* – They recognize that the success and effectiveness of the board and the CEO are mutually dependent and thus partner with the Chief Executive to enhance performance.

2. *Mission driven* – They ensure the connection between decisions and organisational core values by shaping and upholding the mission as well as articulating a compelling vision.

3. *Strategic thinking* – They continuously engage in strategic thinking to sharpen and enhance the organisation's direction by allocating time to what matters most.

4. *Culture of inquiry* – They promote sound, shared decision-making, which is a result of an institutionalised culture of inquiry, mutual respect, and constructive debate.

5. *Independent-mindedness* – They are autonomous and the interests of all facets of the organisation are held above all else for decision-making.

6. *Ethos of transparency* – They ensure that donors, stakeholders, and interested members of the public have access to appropriate and accurate information regarding finances, operations, and results.

7. *Compliance with integrity* – They encourage strong ethics and disciplined compliance. They establish appropriate methods for active oversight.

8. *Sustaining resources* – They connect bold visions and ambitious plans to financial support, expertise, and networks of influence.

9. *Results oriented* – They measure organisational progress towards the mission by evaluating the performance of major programs and services.

10. *Intentional board practices* – They intentionally put structures in place to fulfil important governance tasks supporting organisational priorities.

11. *Continuous learning* – They embrace the qualities of an organisation that is continuously learning. They evaluate their own performance and assess the value that they add to the organisation.

12. *Revitalization* – They invigorate themselves through planned revenue collection, thoughtful recruitment, and inclusiveness of all members.

According to Laughlin and Andringa (2007), eight attributes define good governance in not-for-profit organisations with an excellent board:

1. Division of roles and functions between the board and executive officers while promoting cooperation rather than competition to ensure focus on overall organisational goals.

2. Definition of a self-explanatory mission complemented with good values and functional strategies.

3. Chief executive officer should be highly competent with the skills and capacities for advancing the organisational mission in accordance with the policies setup by the board. The CEO operates under the supervision, but not control of the board.

4. Board chair should be a success-driven individual able to organise and coordinate the board and in doing so ensure the integrity of the board, its structure and processes for managing its roles and duties.

5. Clearly outline the procedures for appointing new board members. For example, elects, orientates, trains, assesses, and establishes a reward system for best performers.

6. Build committees that consult with the board while maintaining their autonomy.

7. Define clear measures to facilitate accountability through legal, financial, and project audits. Promote respect of law, avoidance of conflicts of interest, performance reviews, and self-assessments for board members and staff. This attribute promotes transparency in matters that concern all stakeholders.

8. Promote excellence by ensuring that the board focuses on the principal roles and duties with direct bearing on the organisational purpose.

APPRAISING BOARDROOM PERFORMANCE

According to Cass Bettinger (n.d.) directors should be held accountable for their performance, but that, for the most part, they would welcome a comprehensive accountability driven feedback process.

Jay Conger, David Finegold and Edward Lawler III (1998) in their article *Appraising Boardroom Performance* provide the following reasons why companies should annually review the effectiveness of their boards:

1. Influential investors—in particular, institutional investors—are beginning to demand it.

2. Appraising a board's performance can clarify the individual and collective roles and responsibilities of its directors, and better knowledge of what is expected of them can help boards become more effective.

3. Where board evaluations have been done, meetings have gone more smoothly, there is better information flow, greater influence, and more attention is paid to long-term corporate strategy.

4. Board assessments can also make the relationship between the board and the management better. When formally done, it promotes a healthy balance of power between the board and the CEO. In essence, it becomes hard for a new CEO to dominate the board and avoid accountability for poor performance when the review process is institutionalised.

5. The roles and rewards for directors are changing, and this is creating a compelling reason to regularly review performance. Attention has shifted on corporate governance, and this has made directorships that were initially low-paying and honorary to become more demanding and well compensated. The need for investors is to know what they are getting from the millions of dollars in stock options as well as the cash that their organisations are paying to the directors.

6. Evaluations enable the board and the CEO to hold each other accountable when defining the performance expectations and this

helps to avoid the dangers of getting the board involved in activities that relate to day-to-day management.

7. Evaluations also enhance the board's operations. It explains the roles of the CEO and the board, which ensures that each party focuses on the allocated responsibilities.

Boards have to put objectives in place to enable them to measure their performance (Carver & Carver, 1996). An assessment should make consideration of whether board members get the necessary information prior to meetings that enable them to sufficiently prepare for the meetings they attend, so they can address critical issues. Also, the assessment needs to consider whether the issues being addressed in the meetings are the right issues.

Once an effective board-appraisal process is in place and running, it is a good idea to re-examine it regularly to see how it can be improved or varied to avoid growing stale.

How to Build a Better Board

The infamous collapse of Enron (the US energy company) is a good example of how effective solutions to corporate governance issues must be realised through proper motivation rather than mere emphasis on a checklist for compliance with legal requirements (Brancato, 1997).

The Institute on Governance (2011) provides the following guidelines for strengthening board governance:

1. There is no single solution to all governance challenges. Each challenge is unique based on the model and type of organisation. Organisations are thus encouraged to design governance frameworks that are best suited to their unique attributes (size, norms, culture, internal/external relationships, and background).

2. Have a self-explanatory mission statement reflective of current global events.

3. Have a time-limited organisational strategic plan, which delineates projected achievements within a specified time period such as five years.

4. Source the right skills and expertise for the board. Board success is strongly influenced by the array of competencies possessed by individual members.

5. Ensure a fair and transparent recruitment process for board membership.

6. Have a systematised orientation program for new board members to ensure they are kept abreast of the organisation's standing and future prospects.

7. All employees in the organisation should be encouraged to engage in teamwork in order to overcome challenges. Working together in groups facilitates development of internal relationships as well as organisational culture and helps to mould future leaders.

8. Elect the board chair based on merit and competence. The calibre of the chairperson determines whether the board is headed for failure or success. Equally important, the chair should be an individual with comprehensive knowledge of the core business and processes of the organisation as well as its competitors. Moreover, the chair should be well versed in matters of corporate governance, especially the principle of separation of powers and authority between various management levels. The chair should also show good judgement, be able to amicably and impartially solve board conflicts and differences, and guarantee that the board remains in a position to discharge its duties efficiently.

9. Clear definition of roles, duties, and responsibilities ensures that every employee is aware of the role he/she is expected to play for the achievement of overall organisational objectives. It is also important in mitigating potential conflicts of interest and overlap of duties. Clear job descriptions should be developed for all positions including the CEO, Chair, Vice-chair, and members of the board.

10. Clear demarcation of a position's scope of operation ensures that each one works where they are supposed to.

11. Individual employees at every level should be aware of the scope of their roles and when they become liabilities. For example, using one's positional power to coerce another individual surpasses responsibility and becomes a liability.

12. Good relationship between the board and staff should be developed and maintained. The two areas are interdependent and each group has something to offer the other. Positive rapport between the board and staff is a reflection of democratic corporate governance principles that encourage the board to trust in staff capabilities to deliver without undue pressure.

13. Timely, accurate, and relevant information should be made available to the board. Board members should have access to quality information for planning and decision-making. In addition, planning for board meetings should be carried out with the highest degree of professionalism to ensure that individual members are motivated to attend. Time and information are the two most important components in planning for a board meeting.

14. A comprehensive Code of Ethics should be complemented with a clear policy to address conflict of interest within and outside the organisation. The code of ethics serves as an important guideline for board members to avoid compromising honesty and integrity. It is a key component of good corporate governance practices to positively influence organisational performance.

15. A culture of accountability is achieved through the creation of strong relationships with shareholders and stakeholders. The governing body should exhibit transparency in organisational programs, activities, performance, financial status, and core relationships.

16. Crisis preparedness policy is key in a good governance framework in order to enable the organisation to formulate a pragmatic crisis management policy.

17. Board performance reviews should be routine in order to remind members of their roles, identify weaknesses and strengths and design improvements.

18. Delegation of duties and responsibilities is important so that the board does not do all the work in an organisation but involves other offices while maintaining a supervisory role. Equally important, the board should embrace the concept of good time management exhibiting patience, persistence, and focused leadership.

The Non-profit Genie suggested the following additional ways to reinforce governance and guarantee success.

a) It is important to design structures that place auditors and program evaluators directly under the board in the reporting hierarchy. Firms tend to hire two kinds of independent evaluators: CPA auditors and program evaluators. Despite their independence, these two professionals are selected by the staff and confirmed by the board. In accordance with good governance principles, the evaluators should report to both the board and staff. Equally important, auditors should be appointed by, and should report directly to, the board or a board committee. The provisions of the Sarbanes-Oxley Act (2002) enacted in the USA require audit committees to be directly responsible for the appointment (subject to shareholder approval), compensation and oversight of the registered public accounting firm, including the resolution of disagreements between management and the auditor regarding financial reporting. The auditors are required to report directly to the audit committee.

b) In addition to auditors and program evaluators, boards need unbiased sources of information about management as well. One of the most difficult tasks for boards is the evaluation of the CEO. On one hand, a board can't interview staff about their opinions, but on the other hand, problems are created when a board obtains all its information from the person being evaluated. An independent evaluator might interview staff, and, for example, if there were several allegations of sexual harassment, would report to the board that such charges exist.

c) Good governance should guide board meetings and organisational culture. Board priorities can be classified as governance and support items. Moreover, there should be a transparent reward system for a thorough understanding of dynamic issues, concept articulation, and a participatory attitude. The board should have a culture of tolerance towards contrary opinions and encourage consensus building.

d) The Non-profit Genie further suggested that fair and justifiable board compensation is the first step towards showing the board that their services are appreciated. Performing boards have a right to reasonable compensation for their work regardless of whether the organisation is for-profit or not-for-profit. Reasonable stipends motivate the board to be more accountable and transparent with shareholders and stakeholders about core and non-core activities.

e) Another suggestion for strengthening governance is to recruit a professional and qualified secretary to the board. The position should be created with all necessary benefits. Some organisations and institutions operate with two separate groups of staff reporting to two different authorities within the same firm. Research has established that most boards in not-for-profit organisations are often overstretched in terms of their responsibilities and they lack personal secretaries to delegate some of the non-core responsibilities. A secretary with guaranteed remuneration is key for making the work of the board more efficient and organised.

f) In addition, selecting and recruiting professional governors within the board's array of skills and expertise would be advantageous to have good as well as cooperative subordinates. These increase the competencies of the organisation, which are necessary for accomplishment of organisational purposes and to grow and maintain fruitful relationships. Governors should be individuals with the capacity and motivation to integrate organisational goals with the communities' expectations to have a win-win situation.

At times, there can be stagnation in the relationship between the board and the staff. This is usual and it should not be a cause for alarm. The executive director has different alternatives for handling the problem of re-energizing an existing board (Barine & Minja, 2011).

1) The **direct one-to-one approach** is often effective. The CEO can have private meetings with board members to discuss matters concerning their commitment and interest. Doing this helps the executive to compare the talents and interests of the board members with the tasks they are required to fulfil. Also, it shows that each board member is convinced that every member of the board can perform the essential functions of the organisation.

2) The other way to promote energy in the board is by **training.** Training enables a board to see itself differently. It may be through general instructions about the board members' functions or it may be specific in accordance to the task they will undertake.

3) The board can also be energised by **bringing in new members.** The executive can recommend new members who come in with a new vision and commitment to the company. It can be exciting for the board of directors or the advisory board to work with the executive within the organisation. When legal requirements and political influences are incorporated, there can be a resultant body of individuals that support the projects in the organisation to help it become successful.

CASE STUDY: Prof Chirwa vs The Board on Zambia Railways Limited

Zambia Railways Limited (ZRL), wholly owned by the Government of the Republic of Zambia, is the national railway of Zambia. Incorporated in 1982, its mandate under the Railways Act is to operate both rail passenger and freight trains. It was set up to be the main carrier of mining raw materials and products. Up until 2003, the company was a parastatal but privatised through a concession to a private entity called "Railway Systems of Zambia." The total rail network (2015) is 1,248 Kilometres and stretches from Livingstone in the southern part of Zambia to Chililabombwe in the north. On 10th September 2012, the government rescinded its decision and repossessed Zambia Railways Limited from the private entity due to the general deterioration of the rail infrastructure and rolling stock. President Michael Sata appointed Professor Clive Chirwa as Zambia Railways Limited Chief Executive Officer, replacing

Knox Karima, who retired. This was due to a statement that the President's Special Assistant for Press and Public Relations, George Chellah, issued, "I have deemed it appropriate and opportune to appoint you Chief Executive Officer of Zambia Railways Limited. Your appointment is with immediate effect for a period of five (5) years," read President Sata's letter to Prof. Chirwa in part.

According to the statement made by the head of state, the rail line had deteriorated to the point it could not be described, and the government had terminated the concession to the Railway Systems of Zambia. Furthermore, President Sata explained that it would require much effort to rectify the country's railway line, and this included the inter-mine rail, which played a significant role in the mining sector.

"However, I have confidence in your ability to use your vast reservoir of knowledge to help our country to revamp the railway network that results in a rail system that will create the necessary economic impetus," President Sata stated.

"Government has taken a positive move in this direction by allocating K640 billion for the rehabilitation of the rail line."

Prof. Chirwa was listed as a distinguished Professor of Automotive & Aerospace Structures and Chair of Automotive & Aerospace Engineering, the Editor-in-Chief of The International Journal of Crashworthiness and Advisor to UK, Australia, USA, EU, Japan, Canada and Singapore Gov. on Trans Safety among many other internationally recognized credentials and achievements.

In April of 2013, barely six months into his appointment, allegations were flying left, right and centre on alleged abuse of office and power.

Kaiko Namusa and Chila Namaiko of The Time of Zambia (24th April 2013) reported it this way: ZAMBIA Railways Limited (ZRL) chief executive officer, Clive Chirwa has been suspended for alleged corruption in the manner he managed the national railway. The Anti-Corruption Commission (ACC) has since commenced investigations into reports of alleged corrupt practices and abuse of authority of office against Professor Chirwa and the dissolved ZRL Board of Directors.

The report by Lusaka Chamber of Commerce writer Kevin Esiasa provided the following story.

The impasse between the CEO and the Board of Directors ended up leaving many individuals in Zambia wondering what happened to the operations of ZRL. The events that surrounded Zambia Railways began with mixed information. First, the reports stated that Prof. Clive Chirwa had received a suspension from the company as a result of malpractice. According to Lusaka Times, the company had issued reports that Zambia Railway Board members led by Mark Chona had suspended Professor Chirwa. Also, Lusaka Times reported that the board wanted to do away with Professor Chirwa because he refused to sign their allowances. However, Professor Chirwa dismissed the reports and pointed out the corruption of the board.

According to the statement made by Professor Chirwa as quoted in the Lusaka Times, board members wanted allowances that amounted to KR 500,000, and he refused to sign for the allowances. He then charged the board members that were corrupt. Also, Professor Chirwa alleged that some board members were awarding themselves consultancy services contracts for the organisations they were interested in. Later in the week, other important individuals in government stated that the report explaining the rift in ZRL was exaggerated, and the situation was not as bad as it had been reported. The Minister of Transport, Communications, Works and Supply, Minister Christopher Yaluma, said that Professor Chirwa was still the CEO, and he was not leaving the company despite the differences between the Board and the CEO. Also, the minister stated that it was necessary for Professor Chirwa to remain as RRL CEO so he would revive the organisation's operations. Shortly after that, there were reports of the minister dissolving the entire board of ZRL so investigations could be conducted. According to a report by the Zambia Daily Mail, dissolution took place at a time when reports were circulating concerning financial mismanagement and corruption at Zambia Railways.

According to the Post Newspaper, five members of the Zambia Railways Limited Board Mark Chona, chairman, Professor Oliver Saasa, vice-chairman, and members Geoffrey Mulenga Irene Mbewe and Jonam Mwansa, had differences with Prof. Chirwa, including an attempt to move the company headquarters from Kabwe to Lusaka (incurring ZRL over K72 million monthly rentals without a tenancy agreement). In addition, the Board rejected his demand of US$560,000 annual salary (or K248 million per month) and a 25% shareholding in Zambia Railways at the end of his 5-year contract. This is in addition to demanding a K2.6 billion annual bonus and six free tickets per annum for the wife to UK/Europe. The Board also had an issue with the CEO, Undertaking Rehabilitation of Zambia Railways without Feasibility Studies as well as attempting to use his own company, Clavel Incorporated Limited, to train all senior management staff at Zambia Railways Limited – and without declaring a conflict of interest from the onset. The board members also accused Prof Chiwa of misinforming the nation on the true happenings at ZRL.

In addition to this, the former board chairman accused Prof Chirwa of gross management adding that he tried to undermine the authority of the board on several occasions. Mark Chona said Professor Chirwa must be fired if public resources were to be safeguarded.

As Transparency International Zambia (TIZ) opined, there was a need to challenge other public sector Boards to exercise their fiduciary responsibilities with the utmost care and ensure prudence in the utilisation of public funds. The saga at ZRL was an assault on corporate governance and state house is right to direct investigation in the matter.

Case Study Discussion Questions

1. What relationship issues do you see coming out from this case?
2. Discuss the role of the CEO and the Board as presented in the story?
3. What is your take on the reward system for the board and the CEO for a parastatal in a developing African country like Zambia?
4. If you were the court, what would be your verdict regarding this case and why?

EXERCISE: MEASURING THE EFFECTIVENESS OF YOUR BOARD

Complete the following questionnaire as an individual Director and together as a Board. This exercise should enable you to determine how effective your Board is in achieving its short and long-term goals, managing conflicts and most importantly communicating between itself and its key stakeholders.

Are your Board's short and long-term goals clear?					
Yes/No	If yes, how are they communicated? If no, why not				
Are the combined knowledge and experience of each board member a match to the strategic goals of the organisation?					
Yes/No	If yes, how is that a benefit to the organisation? If no, why not				
How committed to the organisation's vision, mission, organisational culture and values are the board members?					
1 low	2	3 avg	4	5 high	If you rated 1 or 2, how can this be improved
What is the quality of communication among Directors					
1 low	2	3 avg	4	5 high	If you are high, what tools do you use to facilitate this communication?
Do you feel that the board has authority to make decisions independently? (Groupthink influence)					
1 low	2	3 avg	4	5 high	If you rated 1 or 2, how can this be improved
Is the frequency of meetings adequate and is there sufficient time available to prepare for meetings and to deliberate on important decisions while still being time efficient?					
Yes/No	If yes, how has this helped the business? If no, why not				

Are the Board's roles and responsibilities clear?					
Yes/No		If yes, how are they set and communicated? If no, why not			
What is the quality of communication among Directors?					
1 low	2	3 avg	4	5 high	If high, how is this communication facilitated?
What is the quality of the relationship among Directors and Company CEO (if not the same person)					
1 low	2	3 avg	4	5 high	If high, what makes the relationship stand out?
What two actions would you introduce as a director to increase your board's effectiveness?					
1. 2.					

CHAPTER SUMMARY

The relationship established by the board conforms to a top-bottom structure with shareholders at the top, followed by the board chair, directors, and then the CEO. The board forms various committees to be deliberating on various functions at the policy level. These functions may include finance, audit, human resources, and projects among others. There are boards that also have one individual holding the position of the chair as well as the CEO. This combination of roles may compromise the integrity in governance.

A board of directors determines the policy framework and strives to accomplish the organisation's mission and overall goals. The organisational bylaws and/or, the Charter documents and statutes for some organisations serve as guidelines for the board. This chapter also discusses the reasons for conducting board annual performance appraisals. The following reasons provide the rationale for board evaluation:

1. Influential investors—in particular, institutional investors—are beginning to demand it.

2. Appraising a board's performance can clarify the individual and collective roles and responsibilities of its directors, and better knowledge of what is expected of them can help boards become more effective

3. Where board evaluations have been done, meetings have gone more smoothly, there is better information flow, greater influence, and more attention is paid to long-term corporate strategy.

4. Board appraisals may also improve the working relationship between a company's board and its management.

5. The changing roles and rewards for corporate directors create another compelling reason to review board performance regularly. As greater attention has focused on corporate governance, directorships that were once relatively low-paid and essentially honorary positions have become demanding and well compensated.

6. Evaluations create a way for the board and the CEO to hold each other accountable to clearly defined performance expectations while avoiding the dangers of getting the board involved in day-to-day management.

7. Evaluations also improve the operations of the board, clarify the respective roles of the board and the CEO, and ensure that both consistently focus on their responsibilities.

Good governance should guide board meetings and organisational culture. Board priorities can be classified as governance and support items. The board should also have a culture of tolerance towards contrary opinions and encourage consensus building.

CHAPTER DISCUSSION QUESTIONS

1. Explain the issues you would consider to increase board effectiveness

2. Discuss the rationale for board annual performance appraisal.

3. Explain the principles and practices of exceptional and successful boards.

6.

Corporate Governance in Practice

PRINCIPLES AND PILLARS OF GOOD GOVERNANCE

The OECD defines corporate governance principles as having a framework that promotes strategic steering of an enterprise and ensuring process and result-based evaluation of management by the board and additionally, the board's responsibility to the enterprise, shareholders, and community in general (OECD, 2004, p. 17-24).

The Private Sector Initiative for Corporate Governance in Kenya (PSICGK) details good governance as being founded on positive attitudes, ethics, norms, and values reflected in society. Moreover, good governance principles promote accountability for the benefit and welfare of the entire society. Democratic values that support power-sharing, equal representation and participation thrive best in an environment where corporate governance is the norm. The community upholds and appreciates it when its people have a sense of right and wrong, uphold justice and work ethics, embrace technological advancement, and carry out corporate social responsibility. Appropriate employment of available resources is fundamental to the production of goods and services, the promotion of human rights and freedoms, and maintaining security and harmony in society.

According to the Australian Institute of Company Directors, good governance can offer a number of important benefits including:

1. Better organisational strategies and plans;

2. Improved operational effectiveness;

3. More prudent regulatory compliance, financial, and risk management;

4. Improved member and stakeholder engagement and communication flow; and

5. Increased likelihood and degree to which an organisation actually delivers on its purpose.

PSICGK in Kenya developed the code of best practice in corporate governance and identified the following important pillars of good corporate governance:

1) The presence of an efficient, performance-based autonomous body that is at the helm of governance; this body should strive to promote

accountability, efficiency and productivity, transparency and integrity, responsibility, and sustainability.

2) The presence of a well-rounded approach to governance focused on the protection of the rights of all stakeholders and safeguarding their welfare.

3) Governance protocol that outlines management principles preferred by founders of an enterprise and supported by the society as the best way to enhance success.

4) Institutional governance frameworks that encourage and facilitate stakeholders' participation in identifying organisational requirements to achieve goals and resolve problems.

Corporate Governance can be narrowed down to efficiency and effectiveness, accountability, responsibility, transparency, integrity and fairness.

PSICGK has identified the following principles vital for good corporate governance:

a) *Authority and duties of shareholders*: Good governance principles must clearly outline the authority and duties of relevant stakeholders, especially internal members, and facilitate efforts aimed at protecting and preserving the supreme authority exercised in the governance of a corporation. Moreover, corporate governance must provide guidelines for conducting successful general meetings. The shareholders implementing corporate governance are required to exercise authority in the process of sourcing competent and reliable professionals to positions in the Board of Directors to ensure that the corporation gets value. The board should constantly be engaged and have its performance reviewed on a routine basis to ensure that the corporation stays on course. The shareholders in exercise of the supreme authority should also evaluate the board's commitment to the corporation's overall goals through benchmarking its level of accountability and efficiency in the process of discharging its duties. The supreme authority provides for the shareholders' capacity to change the make-up of the board if its performance does not meet expectations.

b) *Leadership*: Running a corporation requires pragmatic and functional leadership that is efficient and effective in the role of steering the enterprise on the path of success. The style of leadership provided by the board is a significant determinant of the level of performance and productivity attained by a corporation at any time.

c) *Appointments to the Board*: The process of appointing the board is crucial in any organisation and should be professionally conducted to ensure that only the most suited individuals are selected to occupy the positions. Prospective board members should be individuals with a capacity to bring value to an organisation through independent decision-making along with other relevant professional skills.

d) *Strategy and Values*: The Board of Directors is responsible for designing and implementing long-term strategies and values that define the purpose of a corporation and ensure its continued growth and sustainability. Moreover, values are encompassed in the public image of the corporation and therefore good values project a good corporate image.

e) *Structure and Organisation*: The board is also responsible for ensuring that the corporation has a practical, functional organisational and management structure. The structure involves the people and systems in a corporation without which it is impossible to realise the overall objectives.

f) *Corporate Performance, Viability and Financial Sustainability*: The board has a duty to monitor and evaluate the design and implementation of strategies, policies, and management performance contracts. The board is also responsible for strategic planning. It is able to assess the sustainability and viability of a corporation's financial standing and this should be done yearly.

g) *Corporate Compliance*: The board should ensure that the enterprise is in compliance with existing laws and regulations, sound governance principles, and accounting and auditing standards that are relevant to its kind of business.

h) *Corporate Communication*: The board is responsible for designing and implementing effective communication channels that encourage and facilitate the participation of various stakeholders in matters important to the enterprise's growth.

i) *Development and Strengthening of Board Member Skills*: It is paramount that board skills and core competencies are regularly reviewed to keep abreast of the corporation's potential challenges as well as future prospects. A policy should be in place to guide on-going strengthening of the skills of the board and other employees to equip them with new knowledge and technologies that are relevant to a dynamic and competitive environment. It is the board's duty to ensure that the corporation keeps pace with other players in the market environment in terms of skills, expertise, information, and technology. Accordingly, the board is responsible for designing a systematic training programme to continually develop its staff.

j)   *Appointment and Development of Executive Management:* The board also plans for the appointment and development of the senior management team. It is mandated to appoint the Chief Executive Officer and other senior management staff. In conjunction with senior management staff, the board implements policies that foster employee motivation as well as protect the corporation's intellectual property. Training programmes should be routine for management and subordinate staff. This is crucial for improving employee productivity and also preparing them for career mobility within the organisation.

k)   *Adoption of Technology and Skills:* The board should also design appropriate frameworks to support the adoption of new technology and skills. The framework must be dynamic enough to accommodate new technologies and knowledge that were not planned for at the establishment of the enterprise. This guarantees the firm's chances for survival and advancement into the future. Moreover, the board must be able to formulate policies that enable the corporation to adopt new technologies and systems that are cost-effective and increase overall performance. Notably, new skills and technology acquired "along the way" renew the corporation's vitality while giving it a competitive edge.

l)   *Management of Corporate Risk:* The board must lead in the formulation of policies for corporate risk management. This requires that it identify and map out potential risk areas and design practical measures to be applied if the risks materialise. The board must also outline identifiable core performance indicators to help in routine benchmarking of the corporation's progress.

m) *Corporate Culture:* Equally important, the corporation eventually develops its own unique culture and the board, with help from senior management, must influence, promote and protect admirable corporate culture traits that align with the entity's purpose and goals. Corporate culture is a compound of practices, ethics, and beliefs that serve as vital anchors for policies, actions, and behaviours in the performance of its core business.

n)   *Social and Environmental Responsibility:* Enterprises have social and environmental responsibilities to society. The board must be at the forefront in ensuring that enterprises meet their responsibilities to external stakeholders by improving the social welfare of the communities around them and protecting the environment. Corporations must strive to integrate with the communities where they operate through initiating and supporting corporate social responsibility programmes which bring about positive impacts.

BUILDING BLOCKS OF BEST CORPORATE GOVERNANCE PRACTICE

A solid governance structure can be supported by four building blocks:

1. Equity among owners;
2. Compliance with regional, national, and international laws and regulations;
3. Governance infrastructure; and
4. Interaction dynamics.

Each of these blocks, when placed appropriately, has a different impact on the benefits the company will engender.

Table 6.1. Applying customised Corporate Governance Approach to Leverage Benefits by Booz and Company

		Benefits Pursued		
		Increased Access to Capital Markets	Maximised Market Perception of Company Valuation	Assurance of Corporate Resilience and Succession
Corporate Governance Dimensions	"Equity" Among Owners	√√√√√	√√√√√	√√
	Compliance	√√√	√√	√√
	Infrastructure (Structure, composition, roles and responsibilities, processes and policies)	√	√√	√√√
	Interaction Dynamics	√	√	√√√

"Equity" Among Owners: investment bank analysts look at the way controlling shareholders are related with other shareholders to promote value creation among the controlling group and benefit all shareholders. When a company fails to follow this principle, it will end up having a corporate governance discount that will lower the value of its shares. In essence, this protects minority shareholders by putting in place the necessary policies and provisions, including fair dividend distribution, proper tag-along mechanisms, having a committed management team, having independent board members, and having a shareholder agreement that has special requirements included.

Compliance: It is the most basic building block because it is a requirement in accessing capital markets. It includes the standards, procedures, and rules when it comes to disclosing essential information to the public. There is a need to control finances, management, and regulate other risks by having the necessary institutions that check and balance at the different levels. The audit committee is one of the tools that can help in this. It is composed of board members and control experts, and its roles include evaluating financial statements before they are released to the public, undertaking ombudsman activities, choosing the right protocols and enacting them, and overseeing internal audits. In this sector, companies have a limited ability for customization since most compliance requirements are set externally.

Governance infrastructure: It is necessary to have a board of directors that functions smoothly and has a strong relationship with the management if the company is to be well-managed. Governance infrastructure helps in determining the governance value. Each company must understand what its needs and business characteristics are before defining its best structure. In the case that companies face scarcity in getting skilled candidates in the short-term, they can have trade-offs between quality and management experience rather than promote independence. This provides one of the ways of tailoring the application of best practices even though it is to happen for a short time. Processes and policies require governance infrastructure, which includes board agenda and the process of making decisions, ethics policies, and board activities flow, among others. When the company's situation is more dynamic and complex, it will require a greater need for board members to be dedicated and efficient in time allocation, which is the primary constraint that boards have.

Interaction Dynamics: The different building blocks each relate to hard elements of governance structure. They ensure that a company complies with the applicable laws and regulations, and that the management infrastructure is well designed. By contrast, interaction dynamics include the soft skills and interpersonal elements that bring together the different pieces to help in the promotion of a coherent system. Depending on the way that the meetings end up being conducted to the ways that the directors' skills and personalities help the company to how the board and management communicate, interaction dynamics helps to promote communication and interpersonal relationships, ensuring that they do not hinder the board's overall health and effectiveness. As the company examines how meetings are conducted, it ends up finding a balance between analysis and decision-making. Furthermore, it is able to calculate the amount of information sharing that occurs and compares it with the counselling needs. This building block also takes into consideration the actual assembly of the board and the skills the company should look for among its board members. The organisation needs to consider the frequency and content of interactions, the access level when it comes to disclosure, and the evaluation tools that the board uses.

These tools and the individual board of directors should be used to promote a productive and collaborative environment. Having the building blocks tailored to match the context of the organisation helps in ensuring that the governance structure ends up being successful as it gets shareholders' approval.

CHARACTERISTICS OF GOOD GOVERNANCE

According to the UNDP (1997) *Governance for Sustainable Human Development,* the following are characteristics of good governance.

a) Participation

All individuals should have a voice in decision-making, whether direct or through institutions that represent their interests. To achieve this, there must be freedom of association and speech, as well as opportunities for constructive participation.

b) Rule of law

Legal frameworks need to be fair and enforced without partiality, especially the laws that deal with human rights.

c) Transparency

Transparency requires the free flow of information to be effective. Processes, institutions, and information are directly accessible to individuals who need them, and sufficient information is offered to promote an understanding and monitor them.

d) Responsiveness

Institutions and processes try to serve all stakeholders.

e) Consensus orientation

Good governance arbitrates differing interests to ensure the board gets to a consensus on the matters that interest the group.

f) Equity

All individuals have opportunities to improve or maintain their well-being.

g) Effectiveness and efficiency

Processes and institutions give results that meet the required needs as they utilise the available resources in the best way.

h) Accountability

Decision-makers in the different institutions are accountable to the public and to institutional stakeholders. The accountability depends on the organisations and whether the decisions are internal or external.

i) Strategic vision

Leaders and the public have a long-term and broad perspective concerning good governance and human development. Also, there is an understanding of complexities in the historical, cultural, and social aspects.

EXERCISE: PRINCIPLES OF GOOD GOVERNANCE CHECKLIST

Use this checklist to confirm whether your current board adheres to the following principles of good governance by PSICGK. You can also list down immediate actions you can do to improve your score.

Principle of good governance	1 (low)	2	3	4	5 (high)
The shareholders of the company have authority to source competent and reliable professionals to the Board without bias or coercion					
The style of leadership from the board is pragmatic and functional towards efficient and effective steering of the company to the path of success					
The process of appointing board members is professional and appointees bring value to the organisation by the skills they possess and independent decision making					
The board is responsible for designing and implementing long-term strategies of the organisation for its continued growth and sustainability					
The management structure is functional and practical					
The board monitors and evaluates the design and implementation of strategies, policies and management performance contracts					
The board ensures that the company is in compliance with existing laws and regulations					
The board skills and core competencies are regularly reviewed and there is a policy in place on board development					
The board has appointed the organisations CEO and senior management team and implements policies that foster employee motivation					
The board is in support of adoption of new technologies and skills					
Board members are able to identify and map out potential risk areas and design practical measures to be applied or mitigate					
The board ensures that the organisation has a thriving social and environmental responsibility programs					

Scores	
45-60	Your board can be rated as following the principles for good corporate governance, maintain this momentum
35-44	Your board is well on its way to being exceptional, keep working
0-34	Your board needs some help in incorporating good corporate governance principles in its running

7.

E-Corporate Governance:
A New Dimension

WHAT IS E-CORPORATE GOVERNANCE?

E-corporate governance involves utilising technology, primarily the internet and related information systems (ISs), to control the activities of other individuals working with the organisation in different positions (Abdennadher & Cheffi, 2020). In essence, e-corporate governance is seen when an organisation utilises technology to guide internal and external interactions. E-corporate governance goes beyond its application in corporations, and it can be used between a government and its citizens. The discipline enhances a government's connection with its citizens by providing a platform where more citizens can interact with the government as the latter puts in the least possible effort. It only needs to build a working system that supports the platform for interaction. It will create the capability to influence and manage citizens' interests, convictions, and practices, among other concepts.

Through e-corporate governance, the government can utilise Information and Communication Technology (ICT) to deliver services to citizens, promote information exchange, and integrate systems between the different parties, such as those between government-to-business (G2B) government-to-citizens (G2C), or government-to-government (G2G).

WHY E-CORPORATE GOVERNANCE?

As a model of governing the different activities that affect an organisation, e-corporate governance is preferable over other forms of governance for various reasons. This section gives the advantages of e-corporate governance to show why it is a preferred form of governance.

E-Corporate Governance offers Reduced Cost of Operation

With e-corporate governance, there is a reduced cost of developing and managing the different individuals involved. To monitor work progress for individuals, one needs the internet and proficiency in information technology (IT). There are no additional costs of operation that come with other forms of governance, such as travelling to different locations to physically meet people associated with the work (Charan, 2010). Instead, one can receive reports over the internet and analyse the performance of the different individuals. Furthermore, customisation in an e-corporate governance system is more accessible than a traditional way of governance where many changes have to be physically made.

E-Corporate Governance Promotes Convenience, Efficiency, and Transparency

When governments use e-corporate governance, it ensures that every individual has an experience that opens them up to opportunities similar to other individuals efficiently and conveniently. In addition, the interest groups, the government, businesses, and individuals can hold each other to account when an e-corporate governance system is used because it provides information to the different parties. Therefore, it reduces issues that relate to fraud, such as specific government officials favouring specific individuals over others.

E-Corporate Governance Platforms are Easily Accessible

In a world that has and continues to experience significant technological advancement, accessing the internet and the services offered across networks has become easier for individuals. In addition, with e-governance, there has been a change in how the government governs citizens. One no longer has to travel to given destinations searching for the services. Instead, they can get these services anywhere as long as they have connectivity to the government's platform to offer these services.

RESPONSIBILITIES THAT COME WITH THE USE OF E-CORPORATE GOVERNANCE

As much as e-corporate governance promotes transparency and efficiency, the users of the platform still have the responsibility of ensuring that they do not abuse the platform. One of the responsibilities of the key players in the use of this system is to have integrity. Both companies and governments must have strong moral principles that guide them to be fair and transparent in their transactions. They should not manipulate the system to work in their favour even when they have the power to do so, but they must ensure that all other platform users get equal services for the same.

The other responsibility of the different users is to promote accountability. When corporations or governments are accountable to other parties, they will do what is right because they know that they are answerable to other parties. Also, the different parties involved with e-corporate governance need to ensure that they make the governance platforms user-friendly. As much as technology has made it possible for more individuals to access the different platforms of e-corporate governance, individuals interacting with these systems need systems whose interfaces are user-friendly to promote better interaction with them.

Else, other users can easily be discouraged from using these platforms. Therefore, it is the responsibility of governments and corporations to ensure that the systems they develop for governance are user-friendly. Other virtues necessary for government and organisations involved with e-corporate governance include punctuality, clarity, accuracy, and comparability.

RELATIONSHIP BETWEEN E-CORPORATE GOVERNANCE AND OTHER DISCIPLINES

E-Corporate Governance and Company Law

E-corporate governance is a practice that has helped in doing away with the old traditional way of operation, and this has made the administration of company law better. For example, organisations no longer have to deal with too much paperwork. At the same time, the administration of company laws is no longer as time-consuming as it used to be. In addition, by increasing globalisation, having sustainable economic growth has been possible for organisations.

An example of a case study where e-corporate governance has promoted efficiency in company laws is in India (Charan, 2010). During the 1990s, the economy of India started growing, and the growth surpassed the techniques used at the time to make government transactions. However, there was a significant lack of transparency and accountability in the country and at the centre of the different corrupt dealings was the Registrar of Companies (RoC). As a result, the implementation of company law was a challenge, which acted as a drawback for corporations.

To help overcome this problem that had persisted for some time, the Ministry of Corporate Affairs sought the use of e-governance in 2006, and it came up with the MCA 21 e-Governance Program. The program started being used for storing all public records, and it helped in bringing about change to the country's corporate affairs. The program has made it easy for stakeholders to access government services without facing different barriers, such as corrupt government officials, which has promoted transparency. As an example of an e-corporate governance system, MCA 21 shows that the effective application of such systems across the world can help bring about lasting change that will be beneficial to the different parties. The various stakeholders that it serves better include:

i. The public. They have improved access to records by corporations, and their issues get addressed effectively.

ii. Professionals. They offer better services than before (Vig, 2012).

iii. Financial institutions. The process and charges involved with registration and verification have been made easier (Praptiningsih, 2009).

iv. Government. They find it easier to govern the country's citizens, and they have a better platform to look at the compliance of individuals and corporations.

v.   Employees. They give the best services to stakeholders.

E-Governance and Corporate Affairs

E-corporate governance has made corporate affairs paperless. Systems that depend on paperwork to operate are limited because paper is a limited resource. By helping to eliminate the use of paperwork in corporate affairs, e-corporate governance has brought about sustainability so that corporations can run in an environment where they are not worried about exploiting resources beyond sustainable measures. The best way for governments and corporations to keep pace with the current needs is to switch to e-corporate governance.

THE HOW OF E-CORPORATE GOVERNANCE

E-corporate governance has the best conditions under which it operates. It needs the parties involved to undertake specific actions to make the implementation of this process possible. The steps that need to be conducted are outlined below:

a) Companies or relevant parties need to send reports through email.

Within the agreed period, organisations or other parties need to send reports through electronic mail to show their performance over the given period. Companies need to be transparent to the point that they should gazette the fact that they are sending a balance sheet to the e-corporate governance system and make it available for employees within the organisation. Doing this will make it easier for government institutions to interact with the different employees working in the organisation.

b) There is an existing law that governs the process of e-governance.

As much as technological advancements are made, and the government and organisations are switching from the old way of governance, the new form of governance still needs to be under the jurisdiction of the law. Therefore, countries must develop laws that determine how industries will operate. In the case of India, an example of this is the companies' bill of 2011. It offers a systematic way for companies to operate under the e-corporate governance so that the country's policies still guide them.

c) The involved parties participate in board meetings.

Whereas systems are changing, different organisations can easily overlook the essence of handling matters officially. To avoid casualness, governments and organisations need to ensure that they still have official meetings that help them run their programs (Jain & Bagga, 2021). Since e-governance is involved with online service delivery, the different meetings can be done through online platforms.

d) There are general meetings done electronically.

Other than meetings that entail the different board members, the involved parties need to ensure that they also hold meetings that accommodate all other involved stakeholders. These can be general meetings held electronically. Through such meetings, individuals can vote for the actions they want the different companies to undertake to make progress.

e) There is the maintenance of electronic books.

To have effective e-corporate governance, companies and governments must maintain records of their information. In addition, good record-keeping on online platforms enhances inspection, which is essential for e-corporate governance.

CONCLUSION

Corporate governance is the way in which organisations are run such that they promote business operations and encourage investors to seek opportunities in supporting the different companies. As this happens, organisations must implement governance procedures that are considered good; otherwise, there will be consequences beyond regulation problems. E-governance comes in as a practice that helps organisations and governments exercise the different procedures of good governance. It needs to be applied in the different industries to promote the virtues that come with it. These virtues include transparency, accountability, and reduced cost, among others.

CHAPTER SUMMARY

In this chapter, the authors argue that good governance is founded on positive attitudes, ethics, norms, and values reflected in society. Good governance principles promote accountability for the benefit and welfare of the entire society. Democratic values that support power-sharing, equal representation and participation in the community upholds and appreciates it when its people have a sense of right and wrong, uphold justice and work ethics, and thrive best in an environment where corporate governance is the norm.

The four building blocks of best corporate governance practice are discussed. Highlighted also are the characteristics of good governance, which include: participation, rule of law, transparency, responsiveness, consensus orientation, equity, effectiveness and efficiency, accountability and strategic vision.

CHAPTER DISCUSSION QUESTIONS

1. Explain the four building blocks of best e-corporate governance practice.
2. Discuss the role of participation in promoting good governance.
3. Explain the characteristics of good governance.

8.

Effect of Corporate Governance on Organisational Performance

According to Lawrence and Marcus (2004), organisations that experience poor governance were less profitable in terms of return on equity, decline in value, and had diminishing economic value in the eyes of the shareholders. The two authors based their conclusions on a study of 2,327 companies. Their study established the existence of a connection between performance and trust-building among and between shareholders and stakeholders. The study employed the 51 corporate governance provisions outlined by the Institutional Shareholders Services (ISS) as parameters for selecting the companies to be studied. The study further established a similarity in the various models of governance principles implemented by different businesses.

The study identified the following four governance styles:

a) **Control-management**, which is established, to produce very good results in organisational performance especially on the sales front.

b) **Trust building** with trust being a valuable component of successful corporate governance that ensures that everybody remains satisfied and happy. Trust ensures that investors and stakeholders will have enough confidence to commit more of their resources to the organisation.

c) **Sovereignty** in relation to the independence of the board and other legitimate authorities to discharge their duties without interference from shareholders, management, or financiers. According to the study, independent boards of governance have a higher chance of steering the organisation towards profitability and improved service or product delivery.

d) **Influence:** Good governance requires that any governing body be free of influence from any quarter. This will ensure prudent running of an organisation especially when it comes to distribution of financial returns.

Shareholders' and stakeholders' confidence in an organisation and its board is largely driven by trust creation and trust preservation. However, overemphasis should not be placed on the aspect of sustaining trust as this would tend to limit personal freedom. Despite trust being an integral part of good corporate governance, it should not obstruct the board from the main purpose of the organisation and associated time limits. The framework for enhancing trust focuses on three main areas: experiential and authoritative sources of trust and strengthening. Furthermore, the three areas can be divided into three more specific categories that include motivation, capability, and risk management.

The different versions of governance identified in the study presented unique patterns indicating varying efforts for establishing and preserving trust within and outside organisations. Trust has a positive relationship with an organisation's valuation. Moreover, poor performance was found in boards that attempted to improve trust by tightening their control. Trust can be built using a variety of approaches but coercion is not one of them. According to William (2006), the board plays an intermediary role facilitating the relationship between the shareholders and management.

FACTORS THAT AFFECT ORGANISATIONAL PERFORMANCE

According to an assessment tool developed by emotional intelligence experts (Organisational Vital Signs) to evaluate organisational performance, there are six principal factors: accountability, collaboration, alignment, trust, leadership and versatility. The variables used in the assessment included customer service, work performance and productivity, and talent retention (William, 2006). The findings of the study indicated the presence of a strong and measurable connection between personal feelings and job performance. In addition, the study established that various groups in an organisation have surprisingly different motivators to perform. The implication was that researchers and leaders could no longer dwell on conventional approaches to appraise performance drivers.

There are 9 key areas that are instrumental for organisational excellence:

a) **Accountable leadership**: presence of a comprehensive structure that facilitates regular review and reporting on performance and organisational relationships.

b) **Core competencies**: the organisation should have sufficient, diverse internal skills and talents that are compatible with strategy and needed competitive advantage.

c) **Control and Coordination**: to ensure that core business activities are running as planned with routine reviews and progress report generation.

d) **Direction**: knowledge of direction reflects knowledge of purpose, two ingredients for success.

e) **Work environment**: characterised by employee interactions (qualitatively and quantitatively), organisational culture, workspace setup, and common understanding of basic organisational values.

f) **Relationships**: an organisation has internal as well as external relationships. External relationships include customers, suppliers, partners, government agencies, and financiers. The handling of external relationships is a major determinant of an organisation's success or failure.

g) **Invention and Innovation**: generally, these terms relate to creation and advancement of new knowledge. An organisation that constantly generates new ideas guarantees its long-term existence.

h) **Leadership**: which appropriately steers and inspires all employees to achieve long-term organisational goals and objectives. Leadership through consultation initiates policies and strategies to improve performance and productivity.

i) **Motivation** involves infusing employees with the desire to perform better through a systematic reward system and conducive work environment.

Assessment should be routine under board supervision to enable members to discern organisational progress towards accomplishing its purpose.

REASONS FOR MEASURING ORGANISATIONAL PERFORMANCE

The formulation of performance measurements serves to ensure that it reaches target levels. However, not all measures are directly related to appraising performance. Some are focused on improving public relations through better communication structures, and in the process improve trust among the board, shareholders, and stakeholders (Behn, 2003). There are eight basic aspects of organisational performance measurement:

a) **Evaluation**: This helps establish the core capabilities of an organisation in relation to overall goals and objectives. Evaluation employs two key variables in analysing performance: organisational performance data and benchmarks. Moreover, benchmarks should have universally acceptable standards to enable comparison of projected against realised and past performance. In addition, standardisation of benchmarks means that an organisation can compare its performance to others in the same industry and the economy at large.

b) **Control:** The traditional control methods exercised by managers in the era of Taylorism (which advocated for standardised procedures in order to conserve investments, sustain the enterprise, and ensure continuous operation and employment) have no place in contemporary management. However, there are still traces of control with some degree of flexibility experienced in human resource management.

c) **Budgeting Process**: This is one of the most crucial processes in any organisation. Organisations can control their performance by employing appropriate budgetary measures. Resource allocation in the budget can be instrumental for improving performance. For example, an organisation may adopt a policy that encourages the allocation of more resources to technological research and development to improve performance. In this way, the organisation will have access to new information and technologies, hence, improved performance.

d) **Work motivation**: The board is responsible for constantly challenging employees to greater achievements. This is done through educating the workforce about targets and established performance measures and linking their achievement to specific rewards; for example, an annual bonus for increased productivity.

e) **Appreciating and celebrating accomplishments**: The governing body should lead people towards a sense of ownership of the milestones accomplished by the organisation. Success is instrumental in solidifying organisational relationships eliciting a sense of togetherness and collective responsibility to keep the "mantle" going. Celebration relieves work pressure so staff can enjoy the fruits of past efforts.

f) **Support**: Plausible performance measurements facilitate verification and validation of success, justification for allocating resources to specific areas, customer acquisition and retention, and securing of shareholder and stakeholder interests.

g) **Learning culture**: This should be an integral part of any success-oriented organisation. No organisation can grow and become successful in isolation. Therefore, the board should design ways of obtaining information about other industry players in an effort to determine which strategies and policies work. Moreover, organisations should always seek new and improved corporate governance practices.

h) **Performance appraisal:** Governing boards should look for the best alternative strategies for improving performance. An organisation may have many departments with varying needs for improvement. Therefore, the board should set priorities based on needs, relevant information, and available resources. In the process of improving performance, an organisation expects to increase accomplishment of its stated mission within the stipulated time frame.

ORGANISATIONAL PERFORMANCE MANAGEMENT SYSTEMS

Various strategies can be employed to improve organisational performance. This includes comprehensive knowledge by the board and management of frequently recurring activities, consistent progress review, and progressive readjustments to cope with the changing global environment while achieving established goals. Good performance management systems have been identified in a wide range of organisations (Ansu, n.d., p.1).

a) **Balanced Scorecard**: This system addresses four main performance indicators - customer perception, internal business processes, learning and development, and financial structure (Kaplan & Norton, 1992). This enhances the process of monitoring organisational progress towards stated goals.

b) **Benchmarking**: Employs standard measurement procedures to compare performance with that of others in the same industry as well as economy. In the contemporary world, players in different industries have come together and designed standard performance benchmarks for their respective industries. This has led to plausible self-regulation in various areas thereby reducing unnecessary interference by government agencies. Standard benchmarking is instrumental in enhancing delivery of quality services and products.

c) **Business Process Re-engineering (BPR)**: Total reconfiguration of an organisation's structures and processes with the aim of raising performance to new heights. The best method to implement BPR is by using a bottom-up approach in the change process.

d) **Progressive Improvement**: This involves gradual and incremental improvement of systems and processes to achieve improved customer satisfaction. This also involves upgrading and removing time barred processes.

e) **Organisational culture transformation**: Cultural change is a far-reaching organisational process that demands commitment of financial, human, and time resources. This change process involves a complete overhaul of organisational norms, value systems, and beliefs.

f) **ISO 9000 certification**: Is an internationally accepted standardisation protocol that provides guidelines to qualify for ISO9000 certification. The protocol is a recognized and internationally respected mark of quality. Its formulation was inspired by the need for uniform, internationally acceptable standardisation.

g) **Knowledge Management:** The concept of knowledge management is a product of information technology advancements. It consists of gathering, organising, and managing knowledge that is critical to organisational growth.

h) **Learning Organisation:** This consists of improving core organisational systems and human resources to raise overall performance and uses systems theory principles to improve performance.

i) **Management by Objectives (MBOs):** The principal focus is to align short-term goals to long-term and overall organisational goals to ensure seamless transitions from one milestone to the next.

j) **Evaluation Based on Outcome:** This is especially important for not-for-profit firms to discover the impact of their activities on target communities. The evaluation process involves outlining projected results to be attained in a target market, and subsequently applying relevant indicators to measure actual outcomes.

k) **Program Assessment:** This consists of evaluation of various applications to establish the best way to improve them: for example, cutting costs of one program to improve the performance of other related programs thus increasing overall performance.

l) **Long-term Planning:** This involves strategic decision-making and is the responsibility of the governing body aided by top management. Long-term planning involves establishment of an organisation's vision, mission, values, and ultimate goals.

m) **Total Quality Management (TQM):** This management practice is aimed at ensuring that customers get the best value for associating with the organisation either commercially or philanthropically.

FRAMEWORK FOR ASSESSING ORGANISATIONAL PERFORMANCE

The International Development Research Centre (IDRC) joined hands with the Universalia Management Group to design and develop a functional framework for self-evaluation by organisations. This framework is designed to provide clarity on key issues such as data collection methods, decision-making models, performance reviews and appraisal, and public image.

The framework narrows the concept of self-evaluation into four critical areas: External Environment, Organisational Performance, Organisational Motivation, and Organisational Capacity.

Figure 8.1. Framework for assessing organisational performance

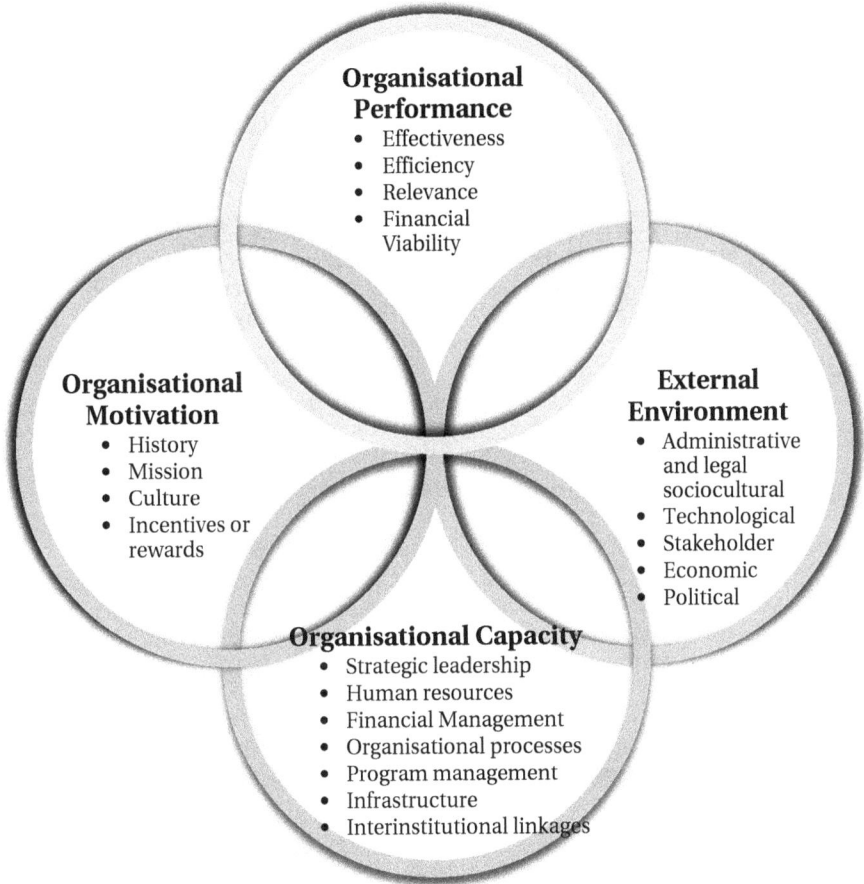

It is possible to tell the performance rating of an organisation by understanding its strategies towards realising its mission. Final products and the impact they have on the target community are the most visible variables used in organisational performance assessment.

Equally important, the concept of performance differs in definition and interpretation over space and time. Interests, knowledge and information available at the time largely influence different interpretations of performance. For instance, administrators might define an organisation's performance in terms of the amount of money brought into the organisation through grants, whereas a donor might define performance in terms of the organisation's beneficial impact on a target group. It is appropriate for each organisation to create its own indicator-monitoring list to suit their direct needs.

The following are examples of organisational performance indicators.

Table 8.1. Example of Select Performance Indicators for an Institution

Category	Indicators
Students	• Social composition • Number of applications for each place • Overall percentage of international students • Percentage of students retained after one year • Percentage of entrants who graduate • Percentage of graduates in employment or further study six months after graduation
Research	• Scores on a national peer review system • Rise in income from non-government sources • Average publications record (or citations) per staff member • Number of commercial spin outs / royalty income • Overall percentage of postgraduates
Staff	• Staff turnover • Percentage on fixed term contracts • Percentage from other nationalities • Proportion of female staff
Finance/Efficiency	• Percentage of income from non-government sources • Percentage of total expenditure on salaries • Financial health/efficiency ratios (reserves/solvency) • Percentage expenditure on building maintenance

Note. Adapted from "Global Trends in University Governance" by Fielden J., 2008, Education Working Paper Series, Number 9, World Bank.

EFFECTIVENESS

In order for an organisation to perform, it must be run effectively and efficiently. IDRC defines effectiveness in an organisation as the degree to which the organisation moves toward the attainment of its mission and realises its goals. However, effectiveness is not a simple concept due to the fact that organisations keep changing their vision and mission statements to suit their interests. Surprisingly, some organisations even condone the "covert" policy of having multiple statements that appear on the organisation's charter and other crucial documents. It is important for an organisation to have a single, incorporating, clear statement that reflects the overall aspirations of the organisation. It is always paramount for leadership to know and understand the organisation's standings in regard to accomplishing its stated mission and goals.

Lusthaus & IDRC (Canada), observe that leadership can achieve this by obtaining the organisational charter, mission and vision statements as well as any other relevant documents. Leadership also needs to ensure that the mission is understood and accepted by all staff and other stakeholders. This will ensure smooth implementation of project activities towards stated goals and objectives. Standard indicators should be used for assessing progress. Also, the leadership should put into place structures and a system to evaluate effectiveness. They should be responsible for supervision to ensure effectiveness in the organisation. Clear, functional communication channels will enhance responsiveness.

The most prominent effectiveness indicators include: clientele base, quality of deliverables, cost-value ratio, environment issues, standard of living, access to basic services and commodities, creation and transfer of knowledge, partnerships and collaborations, policy formulation processes, participants, acceptance of organisational programs by stakeholders, growth benchmarks, frequency of new programs and funding.

EFFICIENCY

This is a core requirement for any organisation to succeed in delivering exceptional products and services at a reasonable price. Efficiency is manifest in cost per service, productivity per employee, and annual cumulative productivity of individual employees. Regardless of their size, performing organisations report impressive returns both qualitatively and quantitatively.

Some key efficiency issues for governance to consider include resource mobilisation, allocation, and utilisation, maximum productivity by individual employees, productive utilisation of physical properties such as plant and equipment, a transparent and prudent financial management system, cost effective administrative and support systems and routinely reviewed performance benchmarks.

Indicators for evaluation and benchmarking purposes include: cost per program, cost per customer, cost-benefit of programs, output (individual and cumulative), and progress towards overall objectives.

RELEVANCE

Organisations develop and change gradually over time and they also experience dynamic metamorphosis along the way. Organisations that survive are those that adapt to changing contexts and capacities and keep their mission, goals, programs, and activities agreeable to its key stakeholders and constituents. Organisations have always experienced internal and external conflicts that can threaten their existence. The strategies each organisation employs to manage crises and avoid foreclosure can make all the difference in their longevity. Along the way, organisations develop a life of their own and need to adapt to a changing environment in order to survive. Some of the issues that determine an organisation's relevance include routine program review for updates and development, mission review and updates, review of shareholder and stakeholder interests, regular review and maintenance of external relationships especially with the community, routine updating of their public image, and creation and adoption of new technologies.

Indicators for measuring relevance include: shareholder and stakeholder satisfaction levels, frequency of new programs, partner sentiment, changes in roles, relations with financiers, rank among other industry players, and rate of adoption of new knowledge and systems.

FINANCIAL VIABILITY

The financial system makes the global economy revolve. This implies that regardless of whether it is a national government or an organisation, it is impossible to survive in the absence of financial resources. In order for organisations to be economically viable, they must have larger cash inflow than outflow. To achieve this, an organisation may have several sources of financing, financial surplus, or constant cash flow.

A guaranteed source of funding that provides stability is critical. Organisations should continually seek new and reliable income sources. They should also improve their productivity to keep expenditures to the minimum while increasing revenue. Organisations must also have contingency plans for unforeseen occurrences. Effective and efficient financial monitoring is equally important and includes monitoring the performance of financiers on other fronts to forestall potential risks.

Indicators of financial viability are composed of the dynamics of net operating capital over a period of at least three years, ratio of outside funds to overall revenues, ratio of available cash to accrued revenues, ratio of current assets to liabilities and total assets to total liabilities, growth in the number of financiers, level of resources mobilised and of diversification of funding sources.

Organisations do not exist within a vacuum but rather must take into account the legal and cultural context of their country of operation. In other words, the external environment can influence how they operate and what they produce. By studying and analysing the external environment, an organisation can better understand the legal, political, socio-cultural, economic, and technological context in which they operate.

THE ROLE OF ETHICS IN CORPORATE GOVERNANCE

Questions of ethics, or the "right way to run a business", are inherent in all aspects of corporate governance and in every board decision and action. Ethical choices are relevant within the core business strategies that boards pursue and the way that they direct the business as a whole to achieve them. According to Julia Casson, business ethics, which can be defined as the application of ethical values to business behaviour, is essentially about the discretionary decisions a board takes to deliver on its duties as set down in law, specified by best practice, and demanded by shareholders and other stakeholders.

The board sets the "tone from the top" of the organisation principally through five means and all these elements need to be in place in order for a board's commitment to ethics to be put fully into practice:

- **Behaviours** – example and leadership
- **Board structures and processes** – appropriate committees, terms of reference and documentation, board/committee interface
- **Purpose, strategy and vision** – what the business will achieve and how
- **Values and standards** – the way in which business will be done
- **Procedures and controls for oversight** – appropriate policies, monitoring and reporting.

Figure 8.2. Ethical aspects of Corporate Governance

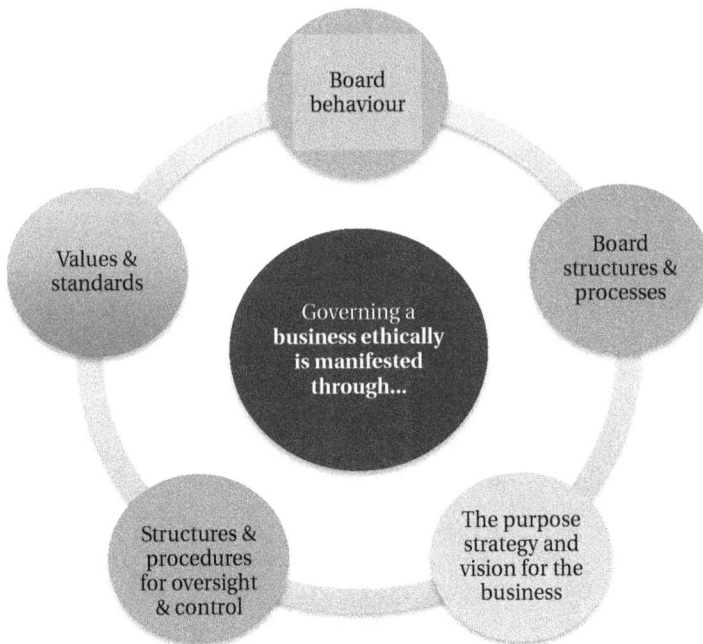

Board behaviours: The board members carry out their duties in a way that reflects ethical values such as integrity, respect, fairness, and honesty.

Board structures & processes: Which facilitate ethical behaviours, avoid unethical ones (such as unmanaged conflicts of interest) and ensure proper accountability - e.g. appropriate board composition, committees, decision-making procedures.

Values & standards: The board articulates and ensures the implementation of the standards of behaviour it expects for business practice, the way business will be done and its role in society (including ethics programmes and CSR initiatives).

The purpose, strategy & vision for the business: The board sets the purpose for the business and what the business stands for; its strategic decisions reflect the business' core values.

Structures & procedures for oversight & control: Mechanisms of delegation and control are conducive to ethical business practice.

ETHICAL CHOICES AT BOARD LEVEL

According to Julia, the five aspects of business practice that should be addressed by any board from an ethics point of view include: diversity, remuneration, accountability, conflicts of interest and transparency

a) Diversity

To promote better diversity on the board begins by having the desire to achieve better decisions by avoiding a board that is composed of individuals who have similar backgrounds or would be inclined to have similar views in addressing specific issues. It is also necessary to avoid board members whose views go unchallenged so that the overall performance can be improved and positively affect the quality of governance (Adams, 2005). Also, there is a strong ethical dimension when it comes to diversity promotion, as ethics like fairness and respect are requirements.

Promoting diversity reduces discrimination against other individuals on basis of cultural, religious, and social aspects.

b) Remuneration

When it comes to business ethics, issues of unfairness revolve around three concerns:

- "Rewards for failure" i.e. the high levels of reward that are paid out to senior employees departing "sinking or damaged ships".

- How executive remuneration relates to pay lower down the organisation, or average employee pay i.e. the gap between the highest and lowest paid

- Low dividend pay-outs and funds applied to long-term investment in the business while executive salaries rise.

c) Accountability

When it comes to ethics and governance, accountability relates with the board being answerable to stakeholders on issues that relate with performance both in the financial and non-financial sectors and the way that performance is achieved. Accountability relates to a two-way process and different companies exert pressure on corporate practice to demand for greater accountability.

d) Conflicts of Interest

Avoiding conflicts of interest helps individuals to avoid seeking personal gain in the different positions they are in within the organisation, which would otherwise put the company at a disadvantage. This is an issue of ethical concern since fairness and honesty end up being absent in cases where there is conflict of interest.

Board members can have conflicts of interest in different ways. Directors may act as representatives for shareholders or other key stakeholders, or there can be an executive director on a unitary board, who would have to conduct executive and governance responsibilities. It is essential for the organisation to recognize such conflicts and manage them ethically so that the director does not profit because of their position. Directors need to be good company stewards and avoid personal gain because they are in a position of trust. This promotes understanding of their roles and responsibilities, which include conflict management and integrity.

Having a personal connection with any part of the business or proposed transaction also promotes conflict among directors. Furthermore, they can have conflict because of the position they hold outside the organisation, which can easily result in withdrawing from board discussions, failing to vote, or failing to take up the steps that the board agrees on.

For the recruitment process to be done effectively, it is necessary for directors to assess the ethical acumen, such as by seeking responses to specific conflicts of interest.

e) Transparency

Transparency is an ethical issue for boards because they need to meet the expectations that the different stakeholders have and promote fairness and honesty in the different practices. The promotion of transparency ensures that stakeholders gain accurate and informed perspectives about the company, whether the perspectives are positive or negative. It limits the extent to which unethical practices get carried out by the organisation. Transparency is also essential when considering the ownership structure of an organisation and the level to which an organisation can identify its stakeholders to promote effective communication and promote the governance of rights. True transparency is not realistic for any organisation where commercial sensitivity is a requirement. However, there needs to be a commitment to "openness" under such circumstances.

CASE STUDY: Scenario 1: CEO x Two

The board of Mongo Publishers, a Nigerian publishing firm hired a new CEO, Ms. Obioma, after going through a period of employee restructuring at the firm. She took over from Mr. Ikechukwu who had served in an acting capacity for two years with no confirmation of the position from the board. Ms. Obioma informed the board that she had recently started her own publishing firm since leaving her previous CEO job in a successful and renowned educational publishing house, Books for Nigeria. The board is fully aware of her business and they see no issue in hiring her as long as she declares that she will not let her business distract from her full time commitment to Mongo Publishers as its CEO. Ms. Obioma's new publishing house (Azikiwe Consultants) deals with the same category of products that she is introducing as part of her job as CEO at Mongo. When she attends Nigeria Publishers' Association (NPA) meetings, she is mainly representing Azikiwe Consultants but using the resources of Mongo Publishers where she is CEO to facilitate her attendance. In the last NPA meeting, members were informed that the government education body would only take on supplementary material from social sciences subjects only. Following that meeting, Ms. Obioma ensures her business adjusts accordingly but does not make mention to the team at Mongo, who go on ahead to spend resources on unnecessary and irrelevant materials trying to comply with government requirements.

Mr. Chibueze is the Production Director at Mongo. In a chance meeting at a mall with a colleague from a rival publishing firm, Babafemi makes a passing statement that he finds it great that this time round the education body was specific in the material they were asking for submission and members can prepare specifically. Mr. Chibueze wonders how come this information seems new to him and why Ms. Obioma did not make any mention of it. He, however, does not confront her as he says the information from Babafemi was not official and perhaps the competing publisher was playing tricks on him. Three months later, it turns out the books they had submitted were rejected and a board meeting was coming up, and for the first time in many years, the company had posted a loss because of the massive investment in a project that did not yield fruit.

Case Study Discussion Questions

1. What Ethical issues, if any, do you see coming out of this case?

2. What would the characters in the case have done differently – the board, Ms. Obioma and Mr. Chibueze.

Scenario 2: Board Chair turned Employee

The current chairman of the University council (or board) of Rayowa Osinachi University, a private university in Lagos, Nigeria, has decided to take on a job as a full-time lecturer and head of department at the university. Mr. Olusegun will report in January when the school academic year begins. As head of department, he will now sit on the senate, which makes academic decisions and reports to the board. The rest of the board members are not aware of Mr. Olusegun's decision and as yet he has not relinquished his position as council chairman. In the December meeting of the board, Mr. Olusegun moves to approve the new university salary scale which doubles the compensation of higher-level employees at the university. The issue of compensation has been an issue because the institution is not financially stable and as a board they had agreed that they should wait for the student numbers to significantly rise before making an overall pay rise to the employees. The current report shows that this has not happened yet. The next board meeting will be in March.

Case Study Discussion Questions

1. What Ethics issues, if any, do you see coming out of this case?

2. Does ethics have a role in corporate governance?

3. As a member of the board, what would be your contribution to the March deliberations?

Note: The cases identified in scenarios 1 and 2 are entirely fictitious and are used only for purposes of discussion. Any resemblance to actual events or persons, living or dead is entirely coincidental.

EXERCISE: BOARD SELF EVALUATION QUESTIONNAIRE

Questions should be answered by all the board members. When completed individually, the results of Sections 1, 2 and 3 should be compiled, shared, and discussed by the whole board to determine an average group answer to each question and an overall section rating. Section 4 should be answered by board members alone but not shared with the group. Sections 1, 2, and 3 should also be completed by the Executive Director or CEO. Section 5 provides feedback to the Chair of the Board.

Tick the response that best reflects your opinion. The rating scale for each statement is: Strongly Disagree (1); Disagree (2); Maybe or Not Sure (3); Agree (4); Strongly Agree (5).

Section 1

How Well Has the Board Done Its Job?	1	2	3	4	5
Our organisation has a three to five-year strategic plan or a set of clear long-range goals and priorities.					
The board's meeting agenda clearly reflects the organizations strategic plan or priorities.					
The board has confirmed that the organisation's one-year operational or business plan exists and is being properly implemented.					
The board has given direction to staff on how to achieve the goals primarily by setting or referring to policies.					
The board is clear on and can articulate (to shareholders etc) the organisation's accomplishments and challenges through the year.					
The board is clear on and can articulate (to shareholders etc) how the organisation has used its financial and human resources through the year.					
The board has ensured that the organisation is in compliance with existing laws and regulations, sound governance principles and acceptable accounting and auditing standards relevant to its core business					

My overall rating (add together the total of the numbers ticked):
✪ Excellent (28+) ✪ Very Good (20 - 27) ✪ Good (15-19)
✪ Satisfactory (12-18) ✪ Poor (7-11)

Section 2

How Well Has the Board Conducted Itself?	1	2	3	4	5
Board members are aware of what is expected of them.					

		1	2	3	4	5
The agenda of board meetings is well planned so that we are able to get through all necessary board business.						
It seems like most board members come to meetings prepared.						
Members receive written reports to the board in advance of our meetings.						
All board members participate in important board discussions.						
Members encourage and positively deal with different points of view.						
Members take a unified stand and support the decisions made as a board						
The board has planned and led the orientation process for new board members.						
The board has a plan for director education and further board development.						
Board meetings are always interesting and frequently fun.						
Members have a commitment to openness and transparency and declare when there is a conflict of interest on any issue discussed in board meetings.						

My overall rating (add together the total of the numbers ticked):
✿ Excellent (50+) ✿ Very Good (40 - 49) ✿ Good (30- 39)
✿ Satisfactory (20-29) ✿ Poor (10-19)

Section 3

Board's Relationship with Executive Director	1	2	3	4	5
There is a clear understanding of where the board's role ends and the Executive Director's begins.					
There is good two-way communication between the board and the Executive Director.					
The board trusts the judgement of the Executive Director.					
The Board provides direction to the Executive Director by setting new policies or clarifying existing ones.					
The board has discussed as communicated the kinds of information and level of detail it requires from the Executive Director on what is happening in the organization.					
The board has developed formal criteria and a process for evaluating the Executive Director.					
The board, or a committee of the board, has formally evaluated the Executive Director within the past 12 months.					
The board evaluates the Executive Director primarily on the accomplishment of the organisation's strategic goals and priorities and adherence to policy.					
The board provides feedback and shows its appreciation to the Executive Director on a regular basis.					

	1	2	3	4	5
The board ensures that the Executive Director is able to take advantage of professional development opportunities.					
There is a mutual respect and supportive relationship between the board and the Executive Director.					

My overall rating (add together the total of the numbers ticked):

✿ Excellent (45+) ✿ Very Good (39 - 44) ✿ Good (29-38)

✿ Satisfactory (20-28) ✿ Poor (11-19)

Section 4 (Not to be shared)

Performance of Individual Board Members	1	2	3	4	5
I am aware of what is expected of me as a board member.					
I have a good record of meeting attendance.					
I read the minutes, reports and other materials in advance of our board meetings.					
I am familiar with what is in the organisation's by-laws and governing policies.					
I frequently encourage other board members to express their opinions at board meetings.					
I am encouraged by other board members to express my opinions at board meetings.					
I am a good listener at board meetings.					
I follow through on things I have said I would do.					
I maintain the confidentiality of all board decisions.					
When I have a different opinion than the majority, I raise it.					
I support board decisions once they are made even if I do not agree with them.					
I promote the work of our organisation in the community whenever I have a chance to do so.					
I stay informed about issues relevant to our mission and bring information to the attention of the board.					

My overall rating (add together the total of the numbers ticked):

✿ Excellent (55+) ✿ Very Good (45 - 54) ✿ Good (32-44)

✿ Satisfactory (20-31) ✿ Poor (13-19)

Section 5

Feedback to the Chair of the Board	1	2	3	4	5
The board has discussed the role and responsibilities of the Chair.					
The Chair is well prepared for board meetings.					
The Chair helps the board to stick to the agenda.					
The Chair ensures that every board member has an opportunity to be heard.					
The Chair is skilled at managing different points of view.					

The Chair can be tough on us as a group when we get out-of-line.					
The Chair knows how to be direct with an individual board member when their behaviour needs to change.					
The Chair helps the board work well together.					
The Chair demonstrates good listening skills.					
The board supports the Chair.					
The Chair is effective in delegating responsibility amongst board members.					

My overall rating (add together the total of the numbers ticked):
✿ Excellent (45+) ✿ Very Good (39 - 44) ✿ Good (29-38)
✿ Satisfactory (20-28) ✿ Poor (11-19)

Adapted from Non-profit Sector Leadership Program, Dalhousie University © 2005

CHAPTER SUMMARY

The authors in this chapter discuss the effect of corporate governance on organisational performance. They argue that organisations that experience poor governance are less profitable and experience diminishing economic value as well.

The chapter discusses the connection between organisational performance and trust-building among various stakeholders. Shareholders and stakeholders' confidence in an organisation and its board is largely driven by trust creation and trust preservation. In addition, factors that affect organisational performance are discussed. These are: accountability, collaboration, alignment, trust, leadership and versatility. The rationale and framework for measuring Organisational performance are also discussed.

The chapter finally explores the role of ethics in corporate governance. Ethical choices are relevant within the core business strategies that boards pursue and the way that they direct the business as a whole to achieve them. Five aspects of business practice that should be addressed by any board from an ethics point of view include: diversity, remuneration, accountability, conflicts of interest and transparency.

CHAPTER DISCUSSION QUESTIONS

1. Explain the relationship between corporate governance and organisational performance.
2. Why is trust important among various stakeholders and how would you create it?
3. Discuss the role of ethics in creating effective governance.
4. Discuss the governance framework used for measuring organisational performance.

9.

Corporate Governance Health Measurement

DETERMINING GOVERNANCE HEALTH

Times have changed and yet the models of governance seem to have remained the same. In an article The Economist of August 16, 2014, titled "Replacing the board: The case for outsourcing company boards" states "Boards are almost exactly as they were hundred years ago: a collection of grey eminences who meet for a few days a year to offer their wisdom. They may now include a few women and minorities. There may be a few outsiders. But the fundamentals remain the same. Board members are part-timers with neither the knowledge nor the incentives to monitor companies effectively." Is it possible to determine if the board of a corporation is asking the right questions? How do you know whether governance is functional or not?

Determining the relative health of a governing body is a complicated process. It's even easier to reduce it to a pass-fail test or create a grade scale based on statistical variables that can lead to a conclusion of either healthy or unhealthy. Diagnosing governance health may be comparable in more ways than one to the practice of medicine. Any physician will consider multiple variables such as test results and other subjective observations to determine a patient's relative health.

How then do you determine whether a governing body is healthy? Is it through a simple process of administering a test, looking through the numbers from the results and comparing them to a universal standard or scale? Or is it a subjective view based on one's understanding of governance issues? Is it determined by comparing an organisation with others either in the same industry or different ones? Is it more important to compare an organisation to its potential in its context? If the approach uses an integrated process with multiple variables, how do you combine and evaluate the data in an objective and fair manner? How do you determine and measure governance health?

A QUANTITATIVE APPROACH TO DETERMINING GOVERNANCE HEALTH

A number of institutions have developed corporate governance indexes with varying focus and coverage. These corporate governance indexes attempt to rank companies by the level of compliance to best practices. Professional rating agencies have come up with various governance rating methodologies capable of measuring the governance scores of companies (Todd, n.d.).

There are several agencies and metrics for the quantitative determination of governance health such as include Governance Metrics International Rating (GMI, 2010), the corporate governance Quotient of the Institutional Shareholders Services (CGQ, 2010), the Corporate Governance Score of Standard and Poor's (CGS, 2010) and the Board Effectiveness Rating (BER, 2010) of the Corporate Library. Most of these rating services depend on publicly available sources of data for developing rating scores. Governance ratings focus on several general categories such as board characteristics, ownership structure, compensation plans, anti-takeover devices, financial closers, internal controls and director education. These aspects included by the governing rating system were analysed by Allan et al. as shown in the table below. What is notable as common practice for many of the rating systems is giving high scores for governance practices that are considered good practices, such as having a high proportion of independent members on the board and high member attendance at meetings, among others, despite the fact that there is no evidence of their contribution to improve company performance.

Table 9.1: Categories of Corporate Governance Rating Systems

	Institutional Share Holder Services (ISS)	**Standard and Poor's (S&P)**	**Governance Metric International (GMI)**	**The Corporate Library (TCL)**
Rating	Corporate Governance Quotient (CGQ)	Corporate Governance Quotient (CGQ)	Governance Metric International (GMI)	Board Effectiveness Rating (BER)
Variable and Categories	61 Variables in 8 Categories	Over 80 criteria in 4 categories	600 Variables in 7 Categories	6 Categories
Number of scores	Overall Plus 8 Categories	Overall Plus 4 Categories	Overall Plus 7 Categories	Overall Plus 6 Categories
Categories				
1	Board structure and compensation	Board structure and effectiveness	Board accountability	Board structure and make-up of skills
2	Executive and Director compensation	Shareholder rights and stakeholder relation	Executive compensation	CEO compensation Contracts and compensation practices
3	Director and officer Stock and ownership	Ownership structure and influence	Ownership base and potential dilution	Outside director shareholdings
4	Charter and by-law provisions	Financial transparency, disclosure and audit	Financial disclosure and Internal control	Ownership

5	Audit		Market for control	Accounting and Audit oversight
6	Take over practice		Reputational and Socially responsible investment issues	Board decision making
7	Director education		Shareholders' rights	
8	Qualitative factors			

Source: Allen et al., 2004, p.40; (Modified)

In contrast to other rating services, Standard & Poor's score corporate governance, the company level governance practices and policies are measured against predetermined corporate governance criteria and related analytical issues which have been developed based on a synthesis of international codes, governance best practices and guidelines of good governance practices. It employs a numeric scale for its corporate governance scores on a 1 to 10 basis with 10 being the best possible score.

The country governance assessment discloses the effectiveness of the legal, regulatory, information and market infrastructure of a country, and it reflects how external forces at a macro level influence the quality of a company's corporate governance.

Table 9.2: Corporate Governance Analytical Framework

Country Analytical Structure	Company Analytical Structure	
Category	Category	Criteria
Market Infrastructure	Ownership Structure and influence of External Stakeholders	Transparency of ownership Concentration and influence of ownership and external stakeholders
Legal Infrastructure	Shareholder Rights and Stakeholder relations	Shareholder meeting and voting procedure Ownership rights, Takeover defences Stakeholder relations
Regulatory Environment	Transparency, Disclosure and audit	Content of public disclosure Timing of and access to public disclosure Audit process
Informational Infrastructure	Board Structure and Effectiveness	Board structure and independence Role and effectiveness of the board Directors and senior executive compensation

Source: Standard and Poor's Governance Services, 2010; (Modified)

An observation made is that the corporate governance scores provide several advantages for various interested parties such as the provision of a systematic overview of all relevant issues of good governance for investors and analysts, a basis for analysing quality of governance; and, a set of scores to investors allowing them to set minimum scores in controlling policy of their general investment portfolio.

Wakasugi et al. of the Japan Corporate Governance Research Institute are credited for the development of the Japan Corporate Governance Index (JCG Index). The JCG index focuses on four main sections: corporate objectives and CEO responsibility; structure and function of board of directors; management system; and, transparency and communication to shareholders. There are seven main governance principles that underlay the JCG Index, namely; governance by the shareholders; clear and measurable corporate goals; a system to assure the responsibility of the CEO and top management team for realising the goals; an independent board with capability to monitor and motivate management; systems for managerial decision-making; implementation, and risk-management; accountability to shareholders by providing timely and sufficient information and securing shareholders' trust through investor relations activities, and; maintenance of transparency through disclosure to all stakeholders. Based on survey responses, the JCG index reports the degree to which a firm adheres to these principles on a scale of 1 to 100 points. They further analyse the relationship between the JCG Index and corporate performance, and find that high JCG Index firms achieved superior performance as measured by ROA, ROE, stock return and employee growth.

The Conference Board Canada (2000) produced "The Governance Index" to rate the boards of companies. This is a self-assessment questionnaire for any board member of a firm to use to rate the effectiveness of the board. Seventeen questions are raised under board responsibility and seven each under independence and effective functioning of the board.

Credit Lyonnais Securities Asia (CLSA) (2001) produced its first report on corporate governance for global emerging markets in 2000. The questions are related to main aspects of corporate governance grouped under seven categories: management discipline; transparency; independence; accountability; responsibility; fairness; and, social responsibility. A composite governance rating is computed by giving an equal weight of 15% to the first six categories and a weight of 10% to social responsibility. The key findings of the study show that there is a high correlation between corporate governance and financial ratios, valuations and share-price performance of companies with larger market capitalization.

It is however important to note that there is no one model of corporate governance that works in all countries as it is a product of political, legal, cultural, and social systems of the country. Having recognized the advantages and relative nature of governance structure, various institutions have made attempts to develop governance indexes suitable for different contextual settings. It is also important to appreciate the limitations for the quantitative approaches to determining governance health. When governance health is measured by statistical data, the results can be misleading if the information is not considered in context of the political, legal, cultural and social systems of the country.

A QUALITATIVE APPROACH TO DETERMINING GOVERNANCE HEALTH

Statistical data is not enough to determine the health of any governance even if viewed in context. A subjective approach must also be considered to determine the health of a governing body.

A subjective approach is likely to be more difficult since it's based on observation rather than simply working with numbers and figures. When leaders are unwilling to critically look at their governance systems, it can lead to overlay optimistic conclusions. It is also subject to manipulation, which is also a possibility for the statistical data. A subjective approach is dependent on the willingness of the governors to ask tough questions and answer them honestly. On the flip side, driven leaders can be hypercritical when using a subjective approach.

Organisational Vital Signs (emotional intelligence experts) have developed an assessment to evaluate organisational performance with six principal factors: accountability, collaboration, alignment, trust, leadership and versatility. The variables used in the assessment included customer service, work performance and productivity, and talent retention (William, 2006). On their part, Smet, Loch, & Schaninger identify 9 key areas that are instrumental for organisational excellence (discussed in an earlier chapter) and which are a reflection of governance health:

1. Accountable leadership
2. Core competencies
3. Control and Coordination
4. Knowledge of direction
5. Work environment
6. Relationships with external stakeholders
7. Invention and Innovation
8. Leadership
9. Employee motivation and reward systems

CORPORATE GOVERNANCE INDEXES

It is important that companies subscribe to corporate governance indices if they are to enhance their corporate governance. The objectives described by the International Bank for Reconstruction and Development (IBRD) and the World Bank motivate organisations to launch corporate governance indices (CGIs).

1. To supplement the legal and regulatory corporate governance framework and thus raise the country's overall corporate governance environment

2. To give companies an opportunity to differentiate themselves in the market

3. To help companies access and tap into an increasing pool of funds committed to good governance and sustainability

According to IBRD, CGIs can be categorised in a number of ways:

- Degree of commitment of listed companies to being part of the index
- Whether the company's evaluation occurs automatically or voluntarily
- Whether there is a cap that limits entry
- Whether only governance or broader environmental, social, and governance (ESG) criteria are evaluated

CODE OF BEST PRACTICES ORGANISATION FOR ECONOMIC CO-OPERATION AND DEVELOPMENT (OECD)

In the OECD annual report for 2005, the OECD described itself as a unique forum providing governments of thirty market democratic countries with a platform to cooperate in the resolution of economic, social, and environmental challenges facing the world today as well as exploit its opportunities (OECD, 2005). The organisation also plays an important role in assisting governments to understand and devise functional ways of adopting corporate governance, information-based economies, and strategies to counter the effects of an ageing population. The forum enables governments to discuss and compare policy experiences, devise solutions to common challenges, and identify and agree on good principles that promote healthy international relations on all fronts.

The organisation was formally established at a convention in Paris on December 14, 1960. OECD's principal objectives include:

- Promotion of strong and stable economic growth, increased job opportunities and standard of living, and transparent and accountable financial systems within member states.

- Assist in the development of plausible economic growth within both member and non-member countries.

- Active participation in the expansion of international trade especially on a multilateral basis while ensuring fairness and justice in shared international obligations.

In December 2000, the OECD had approximately thirty active members. According to OECD, the core elements of plausible governance practices manifest themselves as fair, accountable, responsible, and transparent leadership. The effort to influence the business community to put their trust in investors and good principles of corporate governance has been greatly facilitated by the formulation of the OECD principles of corporate governance (McGee, 2009). In May 1999, the OECD released the original principles of governance. The principles were revised in April 2004 in order to keep pace with the rapid reception of good corporate governance messages especially in relation to investor confidence and national economy performance. In 2006, the OECD Steering Group formulated a mechanism for evaluating how the OECD principles of corporate governance are implemented.

In accordance with various codes and pragmatic models of governance, there are specifically identifiable aspects that define and distinguish good corporate governance practices. Some principles of corporate governance, which are fairly common across borders include:

- *Protection of shareholders' rights and equal treatment:* Organisations should appreciate and protect the rights of shareholders and seek to promote those rights as well as other shareholders' interests. Basic investor rights in a corporation include share ownership, full disclosure of information, voting, and involvement in all decision-making processes.

- *Promotion of all stakeholders' interests:* Legitimate stakeholders have a right to be valued regardless of their level of association with an organisation. It is important that their interests are properly addressed by the relevant authorities.

- *Board roles and responsibilities:* The board should be composed of members with an array of expertise and the capacity to handle challenging business issues to steer management to high performance levels. The board is tasked with the duty of formulating and updating corporate strategy, risk management strategies, executive remuneration and performance appraisals, and ensuring effective operation of the accounting and reporting systems.

- *Ethics and Integrity:* These two values should be high priority for every organisation and drive them towards developing codes of conduct especially for executive and senior management. This guarantees that an organisation's decisions are ethical and promotes integrity in governance.

- *Transparency and disclosure:* Organisations should adopt a policy of openness especially with regard to their purpose and board functions and tasks to improve accountability to shareholders. Procedures should be spelled out to objectively monitor and protect the integrity of an organisation's financial reporting system.

- *Codes of corporate governance:* They help an organisation to be competitive in the market. Other important advantages of governance codes include: provides a conducive environment for discussions for the challenges of corporate governance; facilitates adoption of established and accepted standards of governance; generates easily understandable information for shareholders; provides for routine revision and update of organisational terms of engagement with capital markets. Codes of corporate governance are a set of principles that can only be adopted and implemented on a voluntary basis. These are designed by various entities including stock market authorities, enterprises, institutions, institutional investors, professional associations, and relevant government and international agencies. Codes serve as guidelines for good corporate governance.

CASE STUDY: CAPITAL BANK GHANA

Capital Bank is a wholly owned Ghanaian Bank that was given a class 1 universal banking licence to operate as a Universal Bank effective August, 2013 after operating as a Savings & Loans company since the 29th of October, 2009. On December 1, 2015, the very first step to mark the new forward-thinking approach and the vision to become the local bank of excellence for African markets was marked by rebranding from First Capital Plus Bank to Capital Bank.

Capital Bank's strategic focus is to provide timely and relevant financial solutions to the SME market. Capital Bank is noted for innovation and it's the first financial institution to introduce a deposit solution dubbed; Speed Banking, which makes it possible for customers to deposit cash into their bank accounts anytime, any day, anywhere through their mobile phones without having to visit the banking hall.

In September, 2013, Capital Bank was adjudged the non-bank financial institution of the year 2012 by the Chartered Institute of Marketing Ghana for the company's orientation to marketing & technological innovation, investment in Corporate Social Responsibility and strong financial performance. In October,

2013, it was awarded as the 10th best performing company for the year 2012 and the best in the Non-Bank Financial Institutions sector at the prestigious Ghana Club 100 (GC100) Awards organised by the Ghana Investment Promotion Centre (GIPC).

To actualize the vision that the organisation had, Capital Bank appointed Nilla Selormey to be the consultant who would strengthen the Board of Directors by appointing Mr. Kofi Kwakwa and Mrs. Frances Adu-Mante. Together, they have a combined experience of more than 50 years working for organisations across Africa. The different sectors include private equity investments, banks, corporate strategy development and implementation, corporate governance, entrepreneurship, and law. The board's chairman is Rev. Dr. Mensa Otabil of International Central Gospel Church. The newly reconstructed executive committee is headed by Rev. Fitzgerald Odonkor, who is the managing director. After making these changes, Capital Bank then began a journey to become better in the banking sector, and for five years, it expanded to other African markets. The new capital of about GH¢50 million that was injected into the organisation buoyed it to enable its growth.

As Capital Bank finishes its first year in Africa, it has improved its profile in the Ghanaian banking sector by focusing on customers' retail products, expanding the presence it has across the country, and distributing electronic products that are enhanced to meet the needs of Africans.

In the last year, Capital Bank has partnered with international money transfer providers that are acknowledged for their good services. An example of this is Ria Money Transfer, which has operations in about 147 countries. Integrating the system of Capital Bank with that of Ria enables customers to receive instant payments in the Capital Bank accounts.

In line with the bank's culture of innovation and leadership, it has come up with an innovative solution known as SpeedPay, which enables customers to deposit cash into their accounts anytime and anywhere as they use their mobile phones.

Furthermore, the bank signed an agreement with Allied Oil, the fastest-growing organisation in the petroleum sector. The agreement is meant to make SpeedPay vouchers available to individuals in Allied Oil's service stations. In the past few months, there has been significant success due to this partnership as the bank continues to grow and become more established in the retail sector.

In September, the bank put in place the Young Achiever Account as a means of pursuing superior value and providing holistic financial solutions in the different sectors for its customers. When parents have an initial opening balance of GH¢10 and a minimum operating balance of GH¢100, they can save money towards their children's future. There is an interest of two percent above the savings that an individual has in the bank.

The focus of the bank is on value addition for the different services that it offers as it partners with Africa World Airlines (AWA), a local airline that operates in domestic and sub-regional routes. This enables customers to book flights and purchase Africa World Airlines tickets from the different Capital Bank branches across the nation.

Capital Bank also has 40 sophisticated automated teller machines (ATMs), which enable customers to conduct interbank and intra-bank fund transfer from their Capital Bank accounts to any banks. The customers can use the Ghana Instant Pay platform or the banks internet banking platform. Since the bank has promised to deliver superior value, it has also launched the innovative V-man campaign to get individuals to save more. Customers get free cash vouchers as they open bank accounts with Capital Bank.

Plenty of Awards

The success of Capital Bank not only comes from focusing on the creation of a world-class brand but also from investing in systems, processes, and structures that enable the bank to be more fluid and promote the experiences of its customers. The bank has also invested much in human capital to promote the equipping of staff members and enable the delivery of first-class services that are beyond customer expectations.

The gentle steps of the bank into Africa have been done with good intentions, and they have yielded positive results. The bank was considered the best-growing bank, the best bank in deposits and savings, and the best bank in household and retail banking in 2015. Also, it was considered the best customer service company in Ghana for 2016 by the Ghana Service Council.

In the 2016 Ghana Club 100 Awards, which was organised by the Ghana Investment Promotion Centre (GIPC), the bank was ranked eighth best bank and the 25th best company. The bank is led by a rejuvenated management team, proper business model, sound capital and capital management and good corporate governance.

Looking ahead

After successfully rebranding for a year, Capital Bank remains committed to ensure that the customers have the best solutions with them and the supervisors value Ghanaians as it continues to establish itself across the continent as a brand.

Note. Adapted from http://www.graphic.com.gh/business/business-news/one-year-of-capital-bank-s-africa-journey-to-success.html and http://www.firstcapitalplus.net/about-us/boardofdirector

Case Study Discussion Questions

1. What principles of good corporate governance do you see at play in this case?

2. If you were to rate Capital bank using Organisational Vital Signs evaluation factors of organisational performance, what would be their score?

3. In the wake of many collapsing banks in Africa, what do you think the Capital Bank Board and management should do to continue to thrive?

EXERCISE: MEASURING YOUR GOVERNANCE HEALTH

Indicate where you think on the continuum between excellent, okay and can do better your organisation lies in the following key areas instrumental for reflecting governance health.

	Excellent	Okay	Can do better
Accountable leadership			
Core competences			
Control and Coordination			
Knowledge of company direction			
Work environment			
Relationships with external stakeholders			
Invention and innovation			
Leadership			
Employee motivation and reward systems			

*Note: If you indicated **more than 4 times** between the **okay and can do better section,** your governance **is unhealthy** and should be checked so as to ensure productive continuity of the organisation you govern.*

CHAPTER SUMMARY

The chapter begins a discussion on the current practice in board composition. Boards are composed of individuals who serve a corporation on a part-time basis. These individuals have limited knowledge and few incentives to monitor companies effectively. This begs an answer to a question as to whether many boards are healthy or not. Diagnosing governance health may be comparable to diagnosing a patient in the practice of medicine. Both quantitative and qualitative approaches are used to measure governance health.

A number of institutions have developed corporate governance indexes with varying focus and coverage. These corporate governance indexes attempt to rank companies by the level of compliance with best practices. Professional rating agencies have come up with various governance rating methodologies capable of measuring governance scores of companies.

There are several agencies and metrics for the quantitative determination of governance health such as Governance Metrics International Rating (GMI, 2010), the corporate governance Quotient of the Institutional Shareholders Services (CGQ, 2010), the Corporate Governance Score of Standard and Poor's (CGS, 2010) and the Board Effectiveness Rating (BER, 2010) of the Corporate Library. Most of these rating services depend on the publicly available sources of data for developing rating scores.

Governance ratings focus on several general categories, such as board characteristics, ownership structure, compensation plans, anti-takeover devices, financial closers, internal controls, and director education. Statistical data is not enough to determine the health of any governance even if viewed in context. A subjective approach must also be considered to determine the health of a governing body.

A subjective approach is likely to be more difficult since it is based on observation rather than simply working with numbers and figures. When leaders are unwilling to critically look at their governance systems, it can lead to overlay optimistic conclusions. It also subject to manipulation, which is also a possibility for the statistical data. A subjective approach is dependent on the willingness of the governors to ask tough questions and answer them honestly.

Finally, the chapter argues the importance of companies subscribing to corporate governance indices if they are to enhance their corporate governance. The Code of Best Practices developed by OECD (Organisation for Economic Cooperation and Development) is also discussed.

CHAPTER DISCUSSION QUESTIONS

1. Do you agree with the argument that corporate boards should be outsourced? Give reasons for your answer.
2. Discuss various approaches to diagnosing corporate health.
3. Explain the Code of Best Practices developed by OECD.

10.

Governance in Different Sectors

It has been observed that though principles of good governance may be seen as generic, practices of governance vary from one sector to another due to the unique characteristics of each sector.

GOVERNANCE IN LISTED OR PUBLIC QUOTED COMPANIES

It is generally agreed that weak corporate governance has been responsible for some recent corporate failures in many parts of the world. In order to improve corporate governance, the Securities and Exchange Authorities of various countries have developed a code of conduct for listed companies so as to protect shareholder wealth. These authorities regulate, monitor operations, enhance compliance and advise on other issues that are relevant to promoting good corporate governance practices by public companies. The authorities also help in aligning their practices with international best practices.

When talking of public companies, we are referring to companies having the following two key characteristics:

1. Companies whose securities are listed on a recognised securities exchange market

2. All companies seeking to raise funds from the capital market through the issuance of securities or seeking listing by introduction

Cases of Conflict of Interest

CMC Holding Scandal

On September 6, 2014, The Sunday Nation newspaper produced an article on CMC Holding that shed light on the company having made secret payments to well-connected individuals who served as directors and executives of the company. Details of investigations by the Capital Markets Authority in Kenya and CMC Holdings revealed that prominent personalities had benefited from a mysterious slush fund, an act that constituted illegality.

This slush fund on the English Channel island of Jersey was fed by inflating prices of motor vehicles supplied to CMC. Such an act may have caused customers to pay more to benefit a few individuals. Of particular concern was that CMC is a major supplier to the Government of Kenya, of some of the top range vehicles such as Land Rover and Volkswagen. The inflated prices may have caused taxpayers in Kenya to pay more for no additional value.

According to the investigation report, the price inflation was wired to secret accounts in Jersey as commissions, forming a pool that was paid out to prominent directors and executives from 1997 to around 2013. The money would be paid to individuals as salary top-ups and was made twice a year in Sterling Pounds. Details of payments were disclosed by financial institutions in Jersey, the UK and Switzerland including Regent Trust Co., Royal Bank of Scotland and RBS International.

The scandal at CMC also saw an audit firm, Deloitte, referred to the disciplinary committee appointed by the Institute of Public Accountants of Kenya (ICPAK) after the Capital Markets Authority filed a formal complaint accusing the audit firm of having mishandled CMC's financial statements. The audit firm was accused of having misstated the company's accounts, thereby inflating its earnings. The firm, however, exonerated itself and stated that it relied on the information provided by the management and would not have been able to detect the fraud.

Consequently, the company was delisted from the securities exchange and a foreign firm bought a substantial stake in the business.

Source: Adapted from Sunday Nation, March 18, 2014

Case Study Discussion Question

Discuss the various issues raised in this case that demonstrate the fact the CMC failed to observe good governance practices.

The Fall, the Revival and the Limping of Uchumi Supermarket Ltd.

The company was founded in 1975 as a public limited liability company by three Kenyan parastatal companies - Industrial Commercial and Development Corporation (ICDC), Kenya Wine Agencies Ltd (KWAL) and Kenya National Trading Corporation (KNTC). Uchumi Supermarket Ltd, with branches spread in major towns in Kenya, is the oldest supermarket chain in Kenya. It was established after an agreement was reached between Standa SPA of Italy and the three owners (parastatals). In the agreement, Standa SPA of Italy, then a leading supermarket group with a presence in Europe and vast retail experience, was mandated to manage and train Kenyan personnel who would eventually take over the running of the organisation.

In the 1990's, Uchumi Supermarket spearheaded the hypermarket concept in Kenya. However, in the early 2000's, the company started experiencing financial and operational difficulties occasioned by sub-optimal expansion strategy coupled with weak internal controls. As a result of these problems, the Board of Directors (BOD) on 31st May 2006 resolved that the company ceases operations and subsequently it was placed under receivership on 2nd June 2006. Simultaneously, according to the law governing businesses, the Capital Markets Authority (CMA) suspended the company's listing on the Nairobi Securities Exchange (NSE).

The ensuing scenario after the suspension saw massive redundancies thereby affecting a considerable number of livelihoods both directly and indirectly. Manufacturing firms, which Uchumi Supermarket Ltd worked with closely to promote their products, also registered big losses. At the time, its closure was described as "one of the greatest corporate disasters in independent Kenya history." A government-led rescue plan, however, was initiated and consequently five Uchumi outlets, all in Nairobi, were reopened on 15 July 2006 under interim management and a caretaker administrator.

The government of Kenya and other stakeholders worked out a framework agreement between itself, suppliers and debenture holders and this culminated in the revival of the company. Since then, the management and staff have worked tirelessly to regain its image and place it on Kenya's map of supermarket chains. From a negative bottom line in 2006, the company has reported profits in three financial years i.e. 2012, 2011 and 2010 consecutively. The tremendous improvements led to the leading banks in Nairobi lifting the company's receivership in 2010. By January 2011, the retail chain had returned to profitability and applied to the Kenya Capital Markets Authority to re-list its shares on the NSE. Approval to re-list on the NSE was granted in May 2011 and trading in the shares of Uchumi resumed on 31 May 2011. This happened exactly five years to the date CMA slammed suspension on it.

The supermarket chain announced in 2015 that it was experiencing financial challenges and would close unprofitable branches after it expanded at a rapid pace in recent years. On June 15, the company also dismissed its CEO, Jonathan Ciano and its finance chief, Chadwick Omondi Okumu. It ordered a forensic audit to establish why the company was spending much money yet falling behind when it comes to paying suppliers. "We made an attempt to expand faster than our capabilities and we will be taking a pit stop in terms of branch and country expansion," Sam Oduor stated in an investor briefing. Uchumi opened several branches under Ciano, having outlets in Uganda and Tanzania. In an accusation passed by Oduor, the previous management was said to open new outlets without assessing whether they would profit. "We are looking at this on a case-by-case basis," Oduor said, adding that stores would cease operating if they were not profitable. Uchumi has hired KPMG to conduct a forensic audit for the past two years. "The company is talking to consultancy firms over developing a new corporate strategy, including assessing whether the chain requires an investor from within the industry," Oduor said.

He stated that the past practice where board or staff members were involved with suppliers would stop. "Have we had insiders supplying Uchumi? Yes. Have they been giving us value for money? No," he said, stating that they would eliminate middle men.

Case Study Discussion Questions

1. What issues led to the failure of Uchumi Supermarket?
2. In your view, did the Kenyan government do enough to restore sanity in the company?

Governance Case

How Mumias Sugar was looted dry

The company was founded in 1971 with the following shareholding profile: (a) Government of Kenya (71% shareholding) (b) Commonwealth Development Corporation of the United Kingdom (17% shareholding) (c) Kenya Commercial Finance Company (5% shareholding) (d) Booker McConnel (4% shareholding) and (e) East African Development Bank (3% shareholding) (Michira, 2015). In 2001, the shares of stock of the company were listed on the Nairobi Securities Exchange, where they trade under the symbol **MSC**. The Government of Kenya still retained its position as the single largest shareholder. Beginning in 2012, the company began experiencing lowered sugar output and decreased profits, initially blamed on "inefficiency". The audit firm KPMG conducted a forensic audit. The audit revealed procedural and financial irregularities, which top management had hidden from the company's Board of Directors, leading to a loss of over KSh 1 billion (approximately US $12 million) by the company. These developments led to the firing of 52 top managers, including the CEO, CFO, Commercial Director and Company Secretary. The company also asked the government for KSh2.3 billion (approximately US$26 million) in bail-out funds, of which KSh500 million (approximately US$5.6 million) had been advanced, as of the first week of February 2015. Legal proceedings against the major culprits in the scam also began.

Further revelations indicated that deep after-sale discounts offered to selected distributors, flawed procurement, weak financial controls and importation of sugar contributed heavily to Mumias Sugar Company's financial distress. Management approval allowed Mumias to sell its sugar at below cost, setting the miller on the path to self-destruction. The company that reported Sh 2 billion in net profits in the past and paid over Sh600 million as corporate taxes in its best years was nose diving in and probably on its way to the grave by the beginning of 2015. "There is very little hope that we could ever return it to life after all the plunder," National Assembly Agriculture Committee Chairman Mohamed Noor was quoted by a national daily. This pessimism had been built on several facts.

First, Mumias' accumulated debts were about Sh6 billion in 2015. Secondly, the accumulated losses were fast wiping away the capital. Thirdly, jittery shareholders had already ditched the stock. For example, Abdul Karim Charturbai, the single largest shareholder until late last 2014 had sold his stocks, a response that may have been a representation of many other shareholders. Mr Charturbai was disenfranchised with the management and decided to sell all his 14.4 million shares after it became apparent that the company was no more than a shell. "He was concerned that there was no hope for this company," his personal assistant said in an interview. A company that held so much promise being the single largest sugar producer had been destroyed, she added. Most of Mumias' prospects lay in the new projects that were expected to offer alternative sources of revenue away from sugar. Earlier, Mumias embarked on a massive expansion drive that would eventually see it shift its main milling factory from Western Kenya to the Tana Delta, as it became apparent that sugarcane supply could not support the growing demand. Mumias also branched into co-generation of power from bagasse (the residue after sugarcane stalks is crushed to extract the juice), production of ethanol and even bottled water to widen its revenue base. Lack of willing financiers meant that Mumias could not embark on the expansive sugarcane farming in a joint venture with the Tana River Delta Authority. Mumias, however, would roll out the other expansion strategies with the new product lines.

KPMG's report provided a forensic explanation to the downfall of a behemoth. It emerged that almost anyone in the top management could sign off the massive discounts, as high as 32 percent against a ceiling of eight percent. Requests for these discounts were often raised after the sale had been completed – even in the subsequent months and years. Typically, the contracted distributors would be compensated the equivalent of the discounts through a credit note – a document used to correct an invoicing error. "In certain cases significant credit notes would be raised in subsequent financial years," the audit showed. Over the three-year period starting July 2011, Mumias' 28 top distributors had been granted over Sh2.4 billion worth of discounts. Former managing directors Peter Kebati and Evans Kidero approved the highest value of credit notes. The top distributors handled over 70 per cent of the miller's sugar, the audit pointed out. This meant that Mumias had no control of the retail prices of its own produce in the market. The audit also found multiple cases of conflict of interest where senior officials transacted business with the company, at astonishingly highly inflated costs. Take for instance, the case of a company associated with the Company Secretary which was at one time contracted to carry out fumigation services, taking over from an existing in-house department, at Sh423,000 a month before the cost was revised to Sh1.4 million. The change was attributed to a "correction of a typing error" while the payments would be expedited (Andae, 2015); (Gibendi, 2014); (Wahito, 2012).

Case Study Discussion Question

Discuss the various issues raised in this case that demonstrate the fact the Mumias Sugar Company failed to observe good governance practices.

GOVERNANCE IN NOT FOR PROFIT'S

The process of incorporating these organisations is entirely different from that of profit-making organisations, although this varies from jurisdiction to jurisdiction. This makes the running of these organisations different especially in matters of corporate governance.

The not-for-profit organisations are governed by a board of directors. The size and composition are governed by the organisation's bylaws. While the board has a great deal of authority and power over the affairs of the corporation, there are instances where the chair of the board (who may happen to be a founder) has more power and authority than the board. In effect, such a board serves as an advisory one and does not play a role in providing direction or formulating policies. Such organisations rarely observe good principles of corporate governance.

Although the directors share a legal responsibility to act in the best interest of the organisation and its members, this fiduciary role is silently ignored, particularly in instances where directors see it as a privilege to serve in that board or where the privilege can be withdrawn by the founder.

There are two types of non-profit profit organisations. The first one is the public benefit non-profit making organisations. These carry on activities that are primarily for the benefit of the public. Their revenue sources may include government, public and corporate donations. Such organisations are sometimes referred to as "charities".

Directors of public benefit organisations generally must take into account the interests of a broader range of stakeholders in their decision-making more than directors of the mutual benefit not-for-profit organisations.

The second type of non-profit organisation is the Mutual Benefit organisation. These carry on activities that are primarily for the benefit of their members. They are typically supported by their members through fees and fee-for-service activities or programmes. They may also receive other revenues for specific projects. Such organisations include trade associations, professional societies, golf clubs, social clubs etc.

Elements of Good Governance for Not-For-Profit Boards of Directors

The Panel on Accountability and Governance in the Voluntary Sector chaired by Ed Broadbent in Ottawa, 1999 identified eight tasks required of the boards of charities and public benefit not-for-profit organisations.

1. Steering toward the mission and guiding strategic planning;
2. Being transparent including communicating to members, stakeholders and the public and making information available upon request;
3. Developing appropriate structures;
4. Ensuring the board understands its roles and avoids conflicts of interests;
5. Maintaining fiscal responsibility;
6. Ensuring that an effective management team is in place and oversees the organisation's activities;
7. Implementing monitoring and control systems; and
8. Planning for the succession and diversity of the board.

Governance Case

Founder's Syndrome: Its Influence on Governance practice

James, a long-time executive in an international development agency approached two friends to have the three of them establish a non-government organisation known as Poverty Reduction Foundation (PRF). The three become the primary trustees of PRF. They also agreed to form a board of directors, which led them to incorporate four other people who were experts in development matters. James became the chair of both the board of trustees and the board of directors.

James was highly respected by the board because he contributed to PRF, gaining favour with many development agencies and philanthropists who wanted to be associated with the good work the organisation was doing. The organisation initiated many development projects in several counties, ranging from microfinance programmes to nutrition and eradication of child mortality programmes.

The action of James chairing the two governance organs led him to wield a lot of power over other board members. The chair had a feeling of ownership of PRF which led the board of directors to become a rubber-stamp board. The role of formulating plans, approving budgets, and hiring the chief executive officer and top managers moved from the board to the chair. In many instances, the board did not question the chair's actions and were hesitant to think independently in making decisions for fear of offending the chair.

Five years after the incorporation, cracks started to develop in the board when one director demanded that a forensic audit be conducted on all the projects the organisation had initiated. Three directors and the chair resisted the idea vehemently accusing the director of mistrusting the board. This director finally wrote to the NGO Registration Board asking the governmental agency to cause the accounts and projects to be audited.

The forensic audit was conducted and the findings revealed massive transfer of funds from PRF to the Chairman's personal bank accounts. Consequently, the government instituted legal proceedings against the chair and charged him with fraud and abuse of public trust. The donors stopped funding the projects and the board finally disintegrated.

Case Study Discussion Questions

1. What is "Founder's Syndrome"?
2. Explain how Founder's Syndrome may affect governance negatively.

GOVERNANCE IN THE PUBLIC SECTOR

The framework encourages having a public sector that is better governed and managed, and this is done by improving the process of making decisions and promoting the efficiency of using resources. More effective interventions and better outcomes are promoted by improved stakeholder engagement, robust scrutiny, and overseeing individuals charged with primary responsibility for deciding the direction of the organisation, its operations, and accountability.

Corporate governance includes the processes, customs, laws, and policies that affect the way individuals control a corporation. It also involves the relationship between the different players, who are the stakeholders. Governance is normative. Good governance is brought about by accountability, cohesive practices, and guidance, among other practices. Good governance describes the ways in which institutions need to conduct public affairs and manage public resources.

According to the World Bank, the definition of governance is the manner in which power is exercised in the management of a country's economic and social resources for development. It includes the institutions and traditions through which a country gets to exercise its authority. It looks at the different ways through which governments end up being selected, monitored, and replaced, the capacity of the government to implement sound policies after their formulation, and their ability to respect citizens.

UNDP defines governance as the rules of the political system to solve conflicts between actors and adopt decisions (legality). Governance also helps to describe the way that institutions function and the level in which they are accepted by the public (legitimacy).

Principles of Public Sector Governance

a) **Accountability:** Accountability involves the responsibility that individuals in the public sector organisations have when making decisions and taking actions. Accountability requires all parties to have a clear understanding of the responsibilities for the different parties as well as to understand the defined roles. In essence, accountability is the obligation that the different parties have for the responsibilities they have been given. The responsibilities are wide, including probity, ethics, and the effective implementation of programs.

b) **Transparency/Openness:** This is needed to promote confidence among the stakeholders when it comes to the decision-making process and the actions of the public sector organisations in managing their activities. There is a need for openness by having meaningful consultation with the different stakeholders and offering communication that is clear and accurate, which promotes timely action.

c) **Integrity:** It includes both straightforward dealing and completeness. The basis of integrity is honesty, objectivity, and undertaking actions that are accepted and morally right when it comes to the stewardship of public funds and resources. Integrity depends on the effectiveness of the control framework as it is influenced by the necessary legislation and determined by the professional and personal standards of individuals. Integrity is seen in the decision-making procedure and in the quality of financial reporting.

d) **Stewardship:** Public officials represent the nation. The different resources they use are in trust and not privately-owned. Hence, officials are stewards of the powers and resources they control. Governing public sector organisations is necessary to promote the capacity to serve government and the public interest. Examples include financial sustainability and efficient resource management, together with factors that are less tangible, such as the need to maintain trust in an organisation.

e) **Leadership**: Leadership helps to set the tone and is critical to any organisation.

f) **Commitment to good governance**: This can be added efficiency, which is considered to be a significant resource used to promote an organisation's aims using strategies that are evidence-based. Therefore, efficiency needs objectivity and the merit principle to be applied. For example, when undertaking public business, which includes having public appointments, awarding contracts, or recommending individuals to receive rewards and benefits, holders of public office need to choose on merit.

g) **Specialised Board Committees**: Public entities must establish specialised committees to deal with specific issues such as audit, human resources, risk management, finance operations / technical and where applicable, a corporate governance committee. These committees should be composed of independent directors being the majority.

h) **Board Size and Board Management**: Board of directors should be kept to a reasonable size, since large boards tend to be ineffective. Recognition and utilisation of professional skills and responsibilities among board members must be a critical factor in board management. Governing bodies should include independent directors and preferably should constitute a majority of all directors.
Independent directors should be persons who are willing and able to devote their time to directors' duties.

i) **Due Diligence**: Directors must take time to review important matters to the organisation and establish a record of due diligence. Although directors can engage in constructive criticism, ask tough questions of management at board meetings and disagree with each other, the discussions should be kept collegial with a view to developing a consensus.

GOVERNANCE IN SMALL AND MEDIUM ENTERPRISES (SMES)

SMEs are intrinsically interesting and important. They account for almost half the overall employment in many economies both in developing and developed nations. This highlights the important role these firms play in terms of the dynamics of the global economy. These businesses are responsible for a good number of innovations of new products and processes.

A few unique factors influence their governance practices. A very major one is the size of the firm. Their sizes are important in explaining leverage, risk management, pay-out, board structure and compensation policy decisions.

Another key consideration is that these firms have high operating risks, own assets that are quite firm-specific, and have low levels of transparency.

Small businesses are frequently closely held. They avoid public capital markets and regulatory burdens that come with listing in the capital market. Entrepreneurs also maintain control of the business.

Another unique governance feature is one where there is an overlap between ownership and management. The result is that these firms tend to exploit risky opportunities more extensively than otherwise similar public firms.

Finally, family members seem to compose board membership in many cases and are also part of management. Such board members get compensated as employees and not as directors. If some board members were not part of the family, they would receive too little return on their capital since these businesses rarely declare dividends. The major governance challenge in small and medium enterprises is the separation of ownership and control. Others that quickly follow are the degree of disclosure and availability of data.

Governance Case

Ownership, Control and Business Growth

In 2001, two brothers, Mohindra and Gikera Shah, together with their spouses, started a textile manufacturing firm in Nairobi with an initial capital from family savings of US $250,000. In a period of 3 years, the business had gained a reputation as a high-quality clothing line at very reasonable prices. Due to rapid growth, the four-member board decided to hire two of their cousins to assist in financial and supply chain management.

The business continued to do so well that the board decided to penetrate the entire East African market and consequently appointed distributors for their clothing line in Tanzania, Uganda, and Rwanda.

In 2006, the board decided to open two subsidiary firms in Uganda and Rwanda in order to meet the increased demand and assure customers of a constant flow of their products. They also wanted to avoid delays in delivery that were being experienced in those two countries. To finance this expansion, the firm's directors needed an additional US $500,000. The company's auditors advised the board to go for either a venture capitalist to inject the needed funds or invite new shareholders. The directors argued against that advice because such a move would dilute their control over the affairs of the company. The board finally settled for a short-term debt from a local bank.

The loan was acquired and the company built and equipped the two factories and commenced operations in 2007. During the financial crisis of 2008-2009, the company started to experience working capital problems because the cost of servicing the debt was very high. At the same time, the volume of sales declined as a result of people's purchasing power going down. The board approached the bank to restructure the debt and give the company more time to repay it. This did little to relieve the financial burden. Consequently, the board resolved to scale down the operations by selling one subsidiary company. As the board made this decision, an officer of the auditing firm quipped, "what is the wisdom of forfeiting growth and market opportunities at the expense of retaining control?"

Case Study Discussion Question

If you were invited as a governance expert, what advice would you offer to this company and why?

GOVERNANCE IN FAITH-BASED (RELIGIOUS) INSTITUTIONS

Religious organisations are unusual in their formation and complexity of operations. Many of them are freestanding, self-governing gatherings of believers while others are embedded in formal hierarchies. On the extreme, there are some faith-based organisations that are religious in name only, having no formal ties or accountability to other religious bodies. They are only accountable to themselves with bizarre results at times. This is the case with many charismatic churches in Kenya, which are not accountable to anyone. The self-styled TV evangelists seem to have full control of their congregations even when outsiders see them as outright weird. Operational and financial management issues are in the hands of the founder of the organisation.

The bewildering variety and complexity of religious organisations and service providers offer an opportunity for scholars to examine the corporate governance practices of such institutions. There exists a tension between the expectations of recipients of public funds to be accountable and legal and constitutional protection of sacred companies' autonomy. Religious and other faith-based non-profit organisations have a responsibility of accountability and transparency to their constituents if they are to carry out their missions successfully. These organisations rely on public donations to support their budgets. Support for religious organisations come in the form of tithes, offerings, pledges, planting seeds, etc.

Good governance practices require that boards of management provide a strong framework with adequate checks and balances to cause managers to act in the best interest of their organisations. A unique feature found in faith-based organisations is that leaders and those involved in governance take advantage of their members to enrich themselves and live lavish lifestyles through financial impropriety simply because they are likely to go scot-free, and the membership may not be interested in instituting criminal and legal proceedings against them.

Another unique feature is that the team in charge of financial operations and management has little regard for financial expertise and accountability practices. Leaders of those institutions collect the money, plan for it, and disburse it as they see fit. Unlike public sector and corporate institutions where jobs are clearly defined according to one's area of expertise, this practice is normally ignored in many of these institutions, especially those that do not report to any body or institution of authority.

Financial and operations audit form a critical element of good corporate governance. While you may find financial audits being conducted in formal hierarchical religious institutions, many individual-led religious institutions do not see this practice as necessary. This practice is rampant in countries where the law is not strict on matters of financial dealings by faith-based institutions. An emerging trend in some faith-based institutions, for example, is where constituents are now challenging the church leadership to be more transparent in their operations.

To address governance challenges associated with sacred corporations, governments world over need to pass legislation that is aimed at improving governance in faith-based organisations. In addition, churches themselves should commit to good governance by fundamentally addressing three critical issues. These are:

- Church leadership creates structures that provide fiscal oversight of their operations
- Adequate controls put in place over financial management
- Cases of financial impropriety are being dealt with severely and conclusively.

The following may serve as a guide to improve corporate governance practices of faith-based and non-profit organisations.

1. The founders and / or promoters of those organisations should be separate from management.

2. The organisation should have a governing board with fiduciary oversight responsibility for reviewing and approving the mission, vision, strategic plan, annual budgets, policies, and financial transactions.

3. The organisation should periodically conduct independent audits performed by a Certified Public Accountant. Financial statements should also be availed to membership for scrutiny.

4. The organisation should put in place a code of ethics to be applied by the promoter, the board, and the management of the organisation. Violation of the code of ethics must always be treated as a serious matter.

Governance Case

The complexity of governing in a religious organisation can be demonstrated by the following case.

Tony was appointed Chair of the board of a denominational College that was on the verge of closure due to mismanagement. Appointed together with Tony was a team of professionals whose reputation in their respective industries was beyond reproach, and it was clear that they had their task cut out well for them to get the College back on track.

No sooner had they started their hard work that there was some disquiet in the denomination. The College had a bloated staff, a number of whom were not qualified and had no work to do. However, these members of staff were related to or brought by some of the denominational leaders. It did not help the situation that some of the College administrative staff were part of or had influence in the top decision-making bodies of the denomination and hence could influence the direction and decision of the denomination on the College status.

The board continued with its vision to get the college back on track and hence continued with its work and in the process brought changes that left both the staff and some of the denominational leaders determined to cut short the life of the board. Unfortunately for the board, the principal was very uncooperative and always working against the advice of the board. After several attempts to get the principal to work with the board without success, the board exercised its authority and responsibility and terminated the contract for the principal.

The principal, who happened to have been connected with some of the denominational governing team members, worked behind the scenes, and in the next denominational governance meeting, the board was dissolved, apparently for conflict of interest without a hearing or a chance to defend themselves even though they always kept the senior leadership team of the denomination informed. And with no board to recruit the principal as stated by the College by-laws, the denominational leadership reinstated the previous principal who had been fired for unethical practices and undermining the work of the board.

Case Study Discussion Question

Discuss the various issues raised in this case that demonstrate the complexity of governing in a religious organisation and identify areas where there was failure to observe good governance practices.

GOVERNANCE IN PRIVATE COMPANIES

Serving on a private company board is an attractive option for many, yet it comes with its good share of demands that must be met by each individual director. According to Bruce Golden of Accel Partners, a venture capitalist firm, communication and measurement are the key to good private company governance. Effective communication at board level is crucial because board members understand their role and any known disagreements are worked out early.

Boards are organic systems with people and personalities and there may be conflicts or diverging points of view. Dominant personalities should never be allowed to suppress others' views. It is important in high-performing boards to hear from all relevant voices at the table. Transparency and rapid two-way communication are necessary success factors for any board.

Boards should also develop skills in anticipating issues since business and market dynamics can change rapidly. It behoves boards, therefore, to openly discuss challenges that may likely affect the business. They also must get ahead of situations that can be anticipated with any reasonable analysis. Important issues relating to business should be measured so that boards are able to anticipate change and preempt any negative effects.

Another important aspect to consider is the people who constitute the board. To get the right people on the board, the company should seek out board members who can make a major contribution to the board and the company.

Finally, good boards constantly focus on supporting the development of a strategy for the business. They focus on strategies that will have the greatest impact on the business.

Governance cases in private companies

Profit Padding Ghost Haunts Toshiba

Japan electronics giant Toshiba President Masashi Muromachi announced in a press conference in Tokyo in September 2015 that the company had posted losses of $318 million and drastically reduced its earnings for the past seven years after a scandal in which it was found to have overstated years of profit-making. Toshiba stated that it would reserve a loss of $318 million to account for a scandal that had brought a billion dollars in profit, which made its reputation deteriorate. The announcement has received several delays due to irregularities in the organisation's accounting.

The firm, which has existed for 140 years, stated that its annual loss for the year to March 2015 was $318 million, which was considered catastrophic after the experts' prediction of £1.2 billion in annual profit. The president and vice president of Toshiba left the organisation in July after an independent panel found out that the organisation had overstated its profits for six consecutive years. The estimated profit was a third of what the company had made in profit.

The company was compelled to apologise and promise not to be involved in irregularities in accounting in the future. According to Toshiba, the US had lost some momentum in the second half of 2014 whereas the UK had a stronger performance as the Eurozone had recovered gradually. Although there was a slowdown in China, Southeast Asia and India had solid growth.

Presently, the company has a "management revitalization" committee that negotiates on a new management team. Former Shiseido President Shinzo Maeda will head an 11-member board, and most of these members are external directors. "Toshiba will not announce a FY2015 forecast at this point, as the company continues to carefully evaluate the operational impacts of inappropriate accounting," the firm added.

The organisation's plans will include promoting a faster business selection and concentration and changing the business and financial structures as required. Toshiba is likely to be fined by regulators due to the financial scandal, and this is the biggest in Japan since 2011 when Olympus was involved in a scheme that amounted to $1.7 billion in a quest to cover up more than 20 years of investment losses.

Source: Adapted from: http://www.itpro.co.uk/strategy/25246/toshiba-posts-losses-of-318m-following-profit-padding-scandal#ixzz3lAhBZqKQ

Case Study Discussion Question

Discuss the various corporate governance issues raised in this case.

The Role of Whistle-Blowing in Corporate Governance – Case Study

On 23 October 2014, Tesco Chairman Sir Richard Broadbent came out to say that he wanted to step down. This was after the revelation by Deloitte, a company that conducted independent investigation, that the retailer had overstated its first-half profits by £263m, which was £13m more than what was originally thought to be the case when Tesco announced accounting irregularities on 22 September. It was a whistle-blower and Tesco's GC that brought the attention to the board.

When issues of accounting were first pointed out, Dave Lewis, who became the chief executive of Tesco from the beginning of September, stated "We have uncovered a serious issue and have responded accordingly."

Broadbent and Lewis stated that the investigations had started because an internal whistle-blower had given the information that resulted in the start of discussions about the investigation. This made the retailer's general counsel to go to the CEO with a report, and this led to the start of an investigation. Sir Richard informed analysts that this was "not a failure of financial oversight, this is something out of the ordinary course [of business]."

On 1 October, the Financial Conduct Authority (FCA) informed Tesco that it had begun a full investigation. The situation is also being monitored by the UK's corporate governance regulator and the Financial Reporting Council (FRC). The FRC is empowered to discipline accountants involved in misconduct, and through the Financial Reporting Review Panel, it can ask an organisation to restate its financial statement. On 29 October, the UK Serious Fraud Office stated that it had started a criminal investigation on accounting practices at Tesco. According to Tesco, the overstatement was due to a trading update which took place at the end of August, a time when it gave its biggest profit warning, cut its dividends, and reduced its planned investment. Then, the trading profit – operating profit that is above property gains and losses – for the six months that ended on 23 August 2014, was expected to be around £1.1bn.

Tesco's financial arrangement with suppliers was the cause of the misstatement, and this provided generous credit terms as big grocers wanted to win contracts. The overstatement was "principally due to the accelerated recognition of commercial income and delayed accrual of costs," as well as differences in timing. The focus of the problems was on the UK food business as stated by the organisation.

Crawford Spence, an accounting professor at Warwick Business School, says, "Tesco has essentially tried to recognise revenue too early and delay the recording of costs until a later date. Accounting is not a hard science and some of this behaviour is acceptable, within limits. What Tesco appears to have done is push the boat out a bit too far, ending up with revenue that hadn't really been earned yet and costs that probably should have been booked earlier."

However, Professor Spence adds: "To Tesco's credit, it has flagged this up internally and is doing something about it, which suggests that there are probably no other big accounting shocks hidden away."

Roxana Kahale, founder of Argentinian law firm Kahale Abogados, states that in the case an organisation comes to the knowledge that it is reporting the wrong figures, it is crucial for the organisation to disclose the issue as early as it can and come out as a transparent organisation. "Start an immediate investigation, inform regulators of the issue pursuant to applicable law, retain the assistance of independent counsel and auditors (not the usual outside counsel and auditors), make the appropriate arrangements with press agencies and PR agencies to play out a general communication strategy, as well as separating those parties allegedly responsible for the misstatement pending the investigation," she says.

According to Kahale's beliefs, an in-house counsel has a role that is important in this issue. However, she warns that it is necessary to look into their independence to ensure they have not been involved in the specific incident. Rather, it is better to have an outside counsel with a strong reputation and that is known to handle such kinds of investigations. The in-house counsel can help but they should not take the lead.

According to Kahale's beliefs, Tesco's woes show the need to have effective whistle-blower hotlines, which is a significant role for general counsels as people in the organisation need to be independent so they can pass such concerns to the chief executive.

Often, companies show the essence of having whistle-blower hotlines and protecting the whistle-blowers so the resources can be seen as important ones. Doing this promotes awareness in the organisation concerning its resources so there can be proper control in the company. Boards need to ensure that they stress that there will be no retaliation towards internal whistle-blowers. Also, it needs to outline that there will be no toleration for whistleblowing when it is not made in good faith.

Case Study Discussion Questions

1. How does whistle-blowing enhance the practice of good governance?
2. Are there instances where whistle-blowing may be unethical?

11.

Best Practices: Strategies for Public, Private and Not-For Profit Organisations

Fredrick D. Lipman and L. Keith Lipman (2006) say that good corporate governance helps to prevent corporate scandals, frauds, and potential civil and criminal liability of the organisation. A good corporate governance image enhances the reputation of the organisation and makes it more attractive to customers, investors, suppliers, and, in the case of non-profit organisations, contributors. Below is a summary of major corporate governance principles and best practices according to Lipman and Lipman (2006).

STRUCTURE OF THE BOARD OF DIRECTORS

a) The governing bodies of the different companies (board of directors) need to have an inclusion of completely independent directors, and these directors need to constitute the majority of all directors, except for the case of privately held organisations.

b) Choose independent directors that can devote the required time to undertaking their duties and who are competent to help the organisation and complement other directors.

c) Directors need their own information pipeline into the organisation, which is separate from the information that the management and the independent auditors provide them. This function can also be fulfilled by an internal auditor that reports to the board of directors.

d) The chairman of the board needs to be an independent director except in the case of a private organisation or a case where there is a lead or presiding director. Independent directors need to meet separately from the management directors at least annually. In the case that the board chairman is not independent, the organisation needs to appoint an independent lead or presiding officer.

e) The directors of all organisations need to put in place audit committees, compensation committees, and nominating/corporate governance committees that have independent directors where necessary. Alternatively, these directors should carry out the duties meant for these committees. All board of directors committees should evaluate their activities at least once each year.

f) Organisations, except for small private companies, need to have an internal auditor who directly reports to the board. The auditor should be hired by the audit committee of the board of directors and should be compensated by the same. The internal auditor's primary responsibility should be to help the board of directors with duties that concern the law so they can monitor management. Other duties concerning operations can be assigned to the internal auditors by management.

g) At a minimum, the compensation committee needs to put in place a system that compensates the top officers in the company and use the internal auditor to ensure that the compensation is consistent with what the committee requires of them. Whether alone or with a different nominating/corporate governance committee, it is necessary for the compensating committee to establish the policies of compensation for the company, which need to be consistent with the law.

h) Boards of directors need to be at a reasonable size as large boards are often ineffective.

i) A company needs to have fair opinions from a third party that is qualified and independent in case there is any material transaction that involves a potential conflict of interest. Examples include insider loans, purchase or sale, or material merger or acquisition. Other third parties should not get a percentage of the transaction meant for the fairness opinion.

BEST PRACTICE FOR PUBLIC COMPANIES

a) Public companies need to put in place efficient procedures that enable shareholders to communicate with the board or one of the committees of the company.

b) Board compensation needs to have incentives for directors which make consideration of the long-term shareholder value a section of compensation. Hence, a significant part of the director's compensation needs to be in the form of long-term equity. Directors need to hold the public company's stock for the time that they are members of the board.

c) The board of directors should limit the activities they undertake to oversee the company's management and should avoid micromanagement or day-to-day management activities.

d) Directors must determine the kind of information they require from management to ensure they oversee performance. They must develop metrics that help them monitor management's performance and review these metrics periodically to look at how efficient they are.

e) Directors need to look at the essential issues to the company and record due diligence. When there are transactions that have potential conflicts of interest, it is necessary to form a committee that has independent directors. The special committee needs to record due diligence to promote decisions that are respected by the courts.

f) Directors need to identify major risks, whether directly or through committees. They should prioritise the risks and put internal controls in place as well as compliance programs that help in minimising these risks. Carrying out risk analysis should be used to help develop a committee structure.

g) The board needs to put in place a succession plan for the chief executive officer.

h) The board is obligated to acquire an annual operating plan from management, and this includes annual budgets. Also, it is obligated to monitor the performance of the organisation in accordance with the plan. It also needs to ascertain that the company has a long-term strategic plan and ensure that the plan gets implemented by management.

i) The board of directors and the chief executive officer need to properly understand the different decisions that the management can make without the board's approval as well as those that need the board to approve.

j) When undertaking internal investigations that can require the involvement of top management or be likely to embarrass the organisation, it is a requirement to have an independent board committee (the audit committee) and an independent counsel undertake such investigations.

k) Corporate culture promotes corporate governance. Leadership from the top and a compensation system act as keys to corporate culture. They reward financial performance and provide incentives to employees to report any legal risks. All companies need to adopt a law compliance and ethics policy that helps in enforcing the policies and values of an organisation.

l) It is necessary to establish a whistle blower policy for all companies. They need to publish an employee complaint procedure that promotes confidentiality as one of the policies.

m) All organisations need to adopt a press and media policy that helps individuals with authority to speak on behalf of the organisation. Individual spokespersons need to be trained for this role.

MONITORING AND CHANGING THE CORPORATE CULTURE

a) It is necessary to develop a culture that is ethical and abides by the law for any organisation without having to discourage taking risks on entrepreneurial accounts. The tone at the top of the organisation is a key factor in the establishment of such a culture. The board of directors and management have a difficult challenge in encouraging entrepreneurial risk-taking while discouraging the assumption of material legal risks.

b) Employees must be sensitised to the existing needs of communicating the significant risks to the management and the audit committee.

INTERNAL AUDIT FUNCTION

a) One of the most important actions that can be undertaken in an audit involves the establishment of an effective internal audit function that reports to the audit committee. The internal auditor stands out as the most essential audit committee. Different organisations outsource their internal audit function whereas some organisations have employed staff acting as internal auditors.

b) The compensation committee of the board needs to ensure there are incentives for top management, whether public, private, or not-for-profit, so there can be good corporate governance. The incentives need to include significant economic rewards for the achievement of these goals:

   o Creating an ethical, law-abiding corporate culture

   o Helping the board to come up with an efficient internal control function that overlooks the management of financial statements.

Board committees need to have functions and authority that look at the activities and the major risks that the organisation takes.

SPECIAL COMMITTEES

Special committees are formed for the following reasons, among others:

1. To carry out an investigation that may involve top management or other directors

2. To consider a demand on-a corporation by a shareholder to bring action against other directors and officers

3. To consider whether to terminate an action started by shareholders in the name of the corporation

4. To consider a transaction in which most of the board has financial or other interests adverse to the corporation

5. To consider a transaction where an individual director or the board minority have financial or other interests that will turn out harmful for the corporation, if the director controls the board

6. To consider a transaction where most of the directors get a special or personal benefit that may be incidental to an arm's length transaction if material.

7. To consider a transaction that controls the stockholder such as a going private transaction.

CORPORATE GOVERNANCE FOR FAMILY-OWNED AND OTHER PRIVATE BUSINESSES

- Private companies, including family-owned businesses, can benefit from using independent directors or having the alternative, which is an independent board of advisors.

- Have mechanisms in place that help in dispute resolution in the charter family-owned businesses that are applicable after the death or retirement of the founder.

- Have provisions that promote dispute resolution in the charter of family business, utilising independent directors in the process of dispute resolution after the death of the founder.

- Despite the size, have policies in place that address the different possible conflicts of interest and facilitate the reporting of misconduct by the company managers.

RECOMMENDATIONS FOR CHARITABLE ORGANISATION OR NOT-FOR PROFITS ACTION

- Each charitable organisation needs to review the size of the board after some time to establish the size that is appropriate to promote effective governance and meet the goals and objectives that have been set. All boards need to have mechanisms in place that ensure the board undertakes the required functions and that the members know their legal and ethical roles in ensuring proper governance.

- A board of directors needs to ensure that different individuals hold the positions of chief executive officer, board chair, and board treasurer. If the board considers it necessary for the CEO to also serve as the board chair, the board should have a leader director look into the issues that need a separation of responsibilities.

- The charitable sector needs to undertake a vigorous effort to ensure there is information and education provision to the organisation concerning the roles and responsibilities of the different board members and the factors that the board should take into account when evaluating the size and structure required to have effective governance.

- Whistle-blower policies are essential to defend against fraud.

CHAPTER SUMMARY

The chapter starts by highlighting that good corporate governance helps in preventing corporate scandals, frauds, and potential liabilities for the company. When a corporate governance image is good, there is an enhancement of a good reputation for the organisation, which attracts customers, investors, suppliers, and contributors when the organisation is non-profit. The governing bodies of the different organisations (board of directors) need to have independent directors who should constitute a majority of all directors, and the only exception can be privately-held organisations.

Also, the chapter explains the role of corporate culture in promoting governance. Governors need to put in place ethical, law-abiding culture in organisations while not discouraging entrepreneurial risk taking. A significant element of such a culture is the tone at the top of the company. The balance between encouraging entrepreneurial risk taking and discouraging the assumption of material legal risks is a significantly difficult challenge for the board directors and management.

Appendices

APPENDIX 1: GOOD CORPORATE GOVERNANCE: A CHECKLIST

(Adapted from the Institute of Internal Auditor UK and Ireland Online)

	Yes	No

ORGANISATIONAL STRUCTURES AND PROCESSES

Statutory Accountability

1. Has the board established effective arrangements to ensure compliance with all applicable statues and regulations, and other relevant statements of best practice? ☐ ☐

Accountability for Public Money

2. Has the board established appropriate arrangements to ensure that public funds are:

- Properly safeguarded? ☐ ☐

- Used economically, efficiently, and effectively? ☐ ☐

- Used in accordance with the statutory or other authorities that govern their use? ☐ ☐

Communication with Stakeholders

3. Has the board established:

- Clear channels of communication with the body's stakeholders? ☐ ☐

- Appropriate processes to ensure that such channels operate effectively in practice? ☐ ☐

4. Has the board made an explicit commitment to openness in all the activities of the body? ☐ ☐

5. Does the board:

- Report publicly the processes for making appointments to the board? ☐ ☐

- Make publicly available the names of all board members, together with their relevant other interest ☐ ☐

Roles and Responsibilities

6   Is there a clearly defined division of responsibilities at the head of the body?

☐ ☐

7   Does the board:

- Meet regularly?

- Retain full and effective control over the body?

- Monitor the executive management

☐ ☐
☐ ☐
☐ ☐

8.1. Has the board established a framework of strategic control (or scheme of delegated or reserved powers)

☐ ☐

8.2 Does the framework of strategic control include a formal schedule of those matters specifically reserved for the collective decision of the board?

☐ ☐

8.3 Does the board maintain the framework of strategic control up to date?

☐ ☐

9.1 Has the board established clearly documented and understood management processes for:

- Policy development, implementation, and review?

- Decision-making, monitoring, control, and reporting?

☐ ☐
☐ ☐

9.2 Has the board established formal procedural and financial regulations to govern the conduct of its business?

☐ ☐

10   Has the board established appropriate arrangements to ensure that it has access to all such relevant information, advice and resources as is necessary to enable it to carry out its role effectively?

☐ ☐

11.1 Where the body is responsible for making appointments to the board, has it established a formal process to ensure that such appointments are made:

- In accordance with specified criteria?

- On the basis of merit and the individual's ability to carry out a defined role within the organisation?

☐ ☐
☐ ☐

11.2 Where the body is responsible for making appointments to the board, are such appointments dealt with by the board as a whole?

☐ ☐

12   Is the role of the chairman formally defined in writing?

☐ ☐

13.1 Are non-executive board members:

- Independent of management?

- Free from any other relationships which may materially interfere with exercising an independent judgement on issues of strategy, performance, resources, and standards of conduct?

☐ ☐
☐ ☐

13.2 Are the duties, terms of office, remuneration and its review of non- executive board members defined clearly?   ☐   ☐

14   Where the body is responsible for making appointments of non- executives to the board:

 • Are appointments for a fixed term?   ☐   ☐

 • Are appointments subject to a formal appraisal process?   ☐   ☐

15.1 Does the chief executive have line responsibility for all aspects of executive management?   ☐   ☐

15.2 Is he or she accountable to the board for the ultimate performance and implementation of the board's policy?   ☐   ☐

16   Has the board made a senior executive responsible for ensuring that appropriate advice is given to it on all financial matters?   ☐   ☐

17   Has the board made a senior executive responsible for ensuring that board procedures are followed and that all applicable statutes and regulations, and other relevant statements of best practice are complied with?   ☐   ☐

18   Has the board established a remuneration committee to make recommendations on the remuneration of top executives?   ☐   ☐

FINANCIAL REPORTING AND INTERNAL CONTROLS

Annual Reporting

19   Does the board publish on a timely basis an objective, balanced and understandable annual report?   ☐   ☐

20   Does the board include in its annual report a statement explaining its responsibility for the body's accounts?   ☐   ☐

21   Does the board include in its annual report a statement confirming that it has complied with relevant standards or codes of corporate governance?   ☐   ☐

Internal Controls

22.1 Has the board taken steps to ensure that systems of internal control:

 • Are established?   ☐   ☐

 • Continue to operate in practice?   ☐   ☐

22.2 Does the board include in its annual report a statement on the effectiveness of the body's systems of internal control?   ☐   ☐

23   Has the board taken steps to ensure that effective systems of risk management are established as part of the systems of internal control?   ☐   ☐

24   Has the board taken steps to ensure that an effective
     internal audit function is established as part of the   ☐   ☐
     systems of internal control?

Audit Committee

25   Has the board established an audit committee with
     responsibility for the independent review of the systems   ☐   ☐
     of internal control and the external audit process?

External Auditors

26   Has the board taken steps to ensure that an objective and
     professional relationship is maintained with the external   ☐   ☐
     auditors?

STANDARDS OF BEHAVIOUR

Leadership

27   Has the board taken steps to ensure that its members
     exercise leadership by conducting themselves in   ☐   ☐
     accordance with high standards of personal behaviour?

Code of Conduct

28   Has the board developed a formal code of conduct
     defining the standards of personal behaviour, to which   ☐   ☐
     individual board members and all employees of the body
     are required to subscribe?

29   Has the board established appropriate mechanisms to
     ensure that members and employees of the body are not   ☐   ☐
     influence by prejudice, bias or conflicts of interest?

APPENDIX 2: AREAS OF CORPORATE GOVERNANCE

There are six areas of governance that have been identified by the Institute of Directors in association with Cass Business school. The figure below provides some of the areas that can be used to assess corporate governance.

Figure 12.1. Areas of governance by the Institute of Directors (IoD) in association with Cass Business School, June 2015

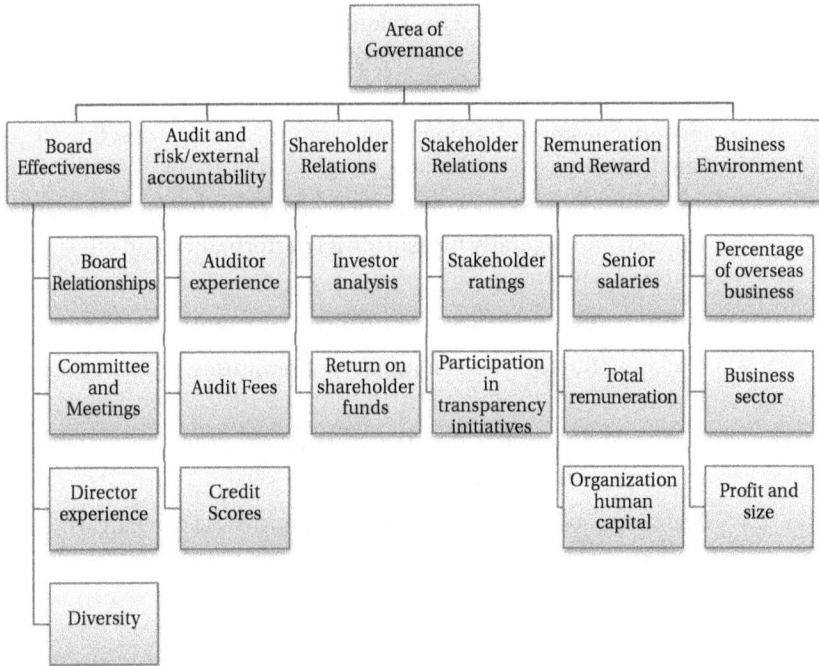

APPENDIX 3: A SAMPLE JOB DESCRIPTION FOR A CHAIRMAN'S POSITION FOR A NON–PROFIT ORGANISATION

The Board Chair will provide leadership to JKL Company and will support and sustain the work of JKL and provide governance leadership and strategic fundraising support.

Specific responsibilities include:

- Developing and managing relationships and communicating with: funders, partners, and other stakeholders

- As a board member, approving JKL's annual budget, audit reports, and material business decisions; being informed of, and meeting all, legal and fiduciary responsibilities

- Reviewing outcomes and metrics created by JKL for evaluating its impact, and regularly measuring its performance and effectiveness using those metrics

- Coordinating an annual performance evaluation of the CEO

- Assisting the CEO and Nominating Committee in recruiting board members

- Periodically consulting with board members on their roles and helping them assess their performance

- Planning, presiding over, and facilitating board and committee meetings; partnering with the CEO to ensure that board resolutions are carried out

- Acting as an ambassador for the organisation

- Ensuring JKL's commitment to a diverse board and staff that reflects the communities JKL serves

Fundraising

- In collaboration with the CEO, generating substantial annual revenue and fostering JKL's overall financial health

- Personally treating JKL as a top philanthropic priority reflected in an annual financial gift

- Ensuring that 100 percent of JKL's board members make an annual contribution that is commensurate with their capacity

- Identifying, qualifying, cultivating, soliciting, and stewarding major individual donors, corporate, and/or foundation gifts

Board Terms

JKL's Board Chair (and board members) will serve a three-year term to be eligible for re-appointment for one additional term. Board meetings will be held quarterly and committee meetings will be held in coordination with full board meetings.

Qualifications

This is an extraordinary opportunity for an individual who is passionate about the success of JKL's beneficiaries and who has a track record of board leadership. The selected Board Chair will have achieved leadership stature in business, government, philanthropy, or the non-profit sector. His/her accomplishments will allow him/her to attract other well-qualified, high-performing board members.

Ideal candidates will have the following qualifications:

- Extensive professional experience with significant executive leadership accomplishments in business, government, philanthropy, or the non-profit sector

- Demonstrated success as a non-profit board member or board chair

- Track record of building credibility in the funding community that has resulted in major gifts to a non-profit

- A commitment to and understanding of JKL's beneficiaries and mission preferably based on experience

- Savvy diplomatic skills and a natural affinity for cultivating relationships and persuading, convening, facilitating, and building consensus among diverse individuals

- Excellent written and oral communication skills coupled with natural affinity for public speaking

- Personal qualities of integrity, credibility, and a passion for improving the lives of JKL's beneficiaries

Service on JKL's board of directors is without remuneration, except for administrative support, travel, and accommodation costs in relation to board members' duties.

Glossary

Accountability
The expectation (of a board) to be answerable to stakeholders for performance, both financial and non-financial, and for the way that performance is achieved.

Advisory board
This is a team that provides direction, counsel and guidance to the governing board, the CEO and other staff, and whose authority is limited to what is granted by the authority point.

Agency theory
A supposition that designates principles (e.g. shareholders) and outlines their capacity to hire the board and management as agents (senior executives and management teams) mandated to steer the growth of an enterprise.

Anglo-American model
A system of governance that is specific for firms from the U.K., but also for those from the USA, Hong Kong and Australia which gives significance to the shareholders' interests and emphasises radical innovation and cost competition while advocating for board independence and its supervision of management's activities for the overall achievement of the organisation.

Balanced scorecard
A measuring system that enhances the process of monitoring organisational progress towards stated goals by addressing these four main performance indicators - customer perception, internal business processes, learning and development, and financial structure.

Benchmarking
The process of comparing the company's products and processes to those of competitors or leading firms in other

	industries to find ways to improve quality and performance.
Best practices	The most successful solutions or problem-solving methods that have been developed by a specific organisation or industry.
Board of directors	A group of people constituted as a decision-making body to ensure the long-term viability of the firm, determine the policy framework and strive to accomplish the organisation's mission and overall goals while at the same time provide oversight of its management team.
Business Process Re-engineering (BPR)	The total reconfiguration of an organisation's structures and processes with the aim of raising performance to new heights.
Chief executive officer (CEO)	The top-ranking person in a business organisation, ultimately responsible for carrying out and implementing the direction, goal and policies, which have been designed or created by the Board, and then reporting on operational outcomes.
Conflict of interest	A situation in which somebody has more than one role and cannot treat them both equally and fairly at the same time.
Continental European (German) model	A system of governance that appreciates the value added to an organisation by employees, managers, suppliers, customers, and the wider community, and based on this premise focuses on securing their interests. The insider-based system is not focused on the strong influence used by active capital markets, but on the existence of strong stakeholders, such as banks and is thus designed to promote innovation and competition.
Corporate governance	The set of processes, customs, policies, laws and institutions affecting the way people direct, administer or control a corporation.

Duty of care	A legal obligation for board members to be active in decision-making and represent the best interests of the organisation and shareholders.
Duty of loyalty	A legal obligation for board members to set aside their personal and professional interests and put the organisation's needs first.
Duty of obedience	The legal responsibility of board members for ensuring that the organisation remains true to its mission and purpose in compliance with all applicable laws.
Effectiveness	The degree to which the organisation moves toward the attainment of its mission and realises its goals.
Efficiency	The quality of doing things well with no waste manifests in cost per service, productivity per employee, and annual cumulative productivity of individual employees.
External governance	An independent system of structures and processes that encompass influences from outside the firm on the governance of the firm – markets, media, unions, laws and regulations.
Governance	A system based on a set of practices to facilitate development of enterprises that are accountable and includes the relationship between exercise of power and management of socio-economic resources for a welfare society.
Governance Excellence Model (GEM)	A system of governance that is represented as a diamond—a GEM—has seven facets or areas of responsibility namely Respect, Reflect, Select, Connect, Protect, Direct, Expect, described as core competency areas for a high-performing institution.
Governing board	The topmost board that has ultimate accountability for the organisation.

Integrity	Comprises both straightforward dealing and completeness and is based upon honesty and objectivity, and high standards of propriety and probity in the stewardship of public funds and resources and management of an entity's affairs.
Internal corporate governance	Encompasses the controlling mechanisms between various actors inside the firm - the company's management, its board and the shareholders.
ISO (International Organisation for Standardisation) Certification	An internationally accepted standardisation protocol that is a recognized and internationally respected mark of quality.
Knowledge Management	The efficient gathering, organising and managing information and resources within an organisation.
Line board	A governance team that serves in place of a single manager and exerts some concrete authority over subordinate authority, but is normally not at the helm of an organisation.
Management	The skill that consists of how tasks, people, resources, relationships, and technology are organised to achieve the overall organisational goal.
Management by Objectives (MBOs)	A management technique whose principal focus is to align short-term goals to long-term and overall organisational goals to ensure seamless transitions from one milestone to the next.
Organization for Economic Co-operation and Development (OECD)	A forum providing governments with a platform to cooperate in the resolution of economic, social, and environmental challenges facing the world today as well as exploit its opportunities. It assists governments understand and devise functional ways of adopting corporate governance, information-based economies, and strategies to counter the effects of an ageing population.

Organizational Performance management	An ongoing process of communication created to appraise performance and includes comprehensive knowledge by the board and management of frequently recurring activities, consistent progress review, and progressive readjustments to cope with the changing global environment while achieving established goals.
Policy governance model	A system of governance that proposes that the role of the board is to add value to the interests of the shareholders rather than to be concerned with the welfare of managers and thus the main responsibility of the board is inspired by the owner-representative accountability principle and the need to delegate more power to management.
Political theory	A democratic and transparent system that demands vote support from shareholders. The government is the guardian of public interest in the process of corporate decision-making especially with respect to specific cultural experiences.
Program Assessment	The evaluation of various applications to establish the best way to improve them.
Progressive Improvement	The gradual and incremental improvement of systems and processes to achieve improved customer satisfaction.
Resource dependency theory	A supposition that explains governance as a rationalisation of the board, its role in allocating resources to the firm, and its overall mandate.
Risk governance	The oversight of critical risks and risk decisions made by an organisation.
Risk management	The forecasting and evaluation of financial risks together with the identification of procedures to avoid or minimise their impact. It is the oversight of enterprise risk programs in an organisation.

Shareholders	Owners of shares in a company or business.
Stakeholder theory	An organisation management supposition that focuses on the group or person (management, suppliers, employees, and business partners) whose relationship with the organisation is a product of the organisational goals and objectives.
Stakeholders	The workforce, suppliers, customers, financial institutions, and regulators as well as the surrounding community within the corporate governance structure.
Stewardship theory	An organisation management supposition that assumes that stewards, notably, top management are responsible for the protection and augmentation of shareholders' wealth through high productivity and performance and will derive both satisfaction and motivation from the organisation's successful performance.
Total Quality Management (TQM)	Programs designed to constantly improve the quality of products, services and marketing processes.
Transaction cost theory	A proposition that governance is an interdisciplinary integration of law, economics, and organisation, which uses transactions as the preferred unit of analysis and sees the firm as an entity that accommodates people with varying views and objectives.
Transparency	The condition of donors, stakeholders, and interested members of the public having access to appropriate and accurate information regarding finances, operations, and results of an organisation.
Whistle-blower	A person who informs on a person or organisation regarded as engaging in an unlawful or immoral activity.

Working group board   This is a governing group with few or no subordinates or staff and thus the board both governs and works.

Bibliography

Adams, O. (2005). Quality of Board Governance in Not-for-profit Healthcare Organisations. *The Internet Journal of Healthcare Administration 2* (2). https://doi.org/10.5580/251d

American Society for Training and Development. (2005). *Organisational Climate Helps Predict Performance.* http://findarticles.com/p/articles/mi_m4467/is_200506/ai_n21373248/

Andae, G. (2015, February 3). *Mumias Suspends 52 Top Employees Over Loss of KSh400 Million.* Business Daily Africa https://www.businessdailyafrica.com/Corporate-News/Mumias-Sugar-suspends-52-top-employees/-/539550/2612056/-/p00dln/-/index.html

Ansu, A. (n.d.). *Examples of Organisational Performance Management Systems.* Retrieved from http://www.scribd.com/doc/44220199/Examples-of-Organizational-Performance-Management-Systems

Argenti, J. (1993). *Your Organisation: What Is It For?* London: McGraw-Hill.

Avellaneda, S. (2010). Good Governance, Institutions and Economic Development: Beyond the Conventional Wisdom. *British Journal Of Political Science, 40*(1), 195-224. Retrieved 22 July 2022.

Baker, H. K., & Anderson, R. (2010). *Corporate governance: A synthesis of theory, research, and practice.* Hoboken, N.J: John Wiley & Sons.

Barine, K., & Minja, D. (2010). *Transformational Corporate Leadership.* Wake Forest: Integrity Publishers Inc.

Behn, R. (2003). Why Measure Performance? Different Purposes Require Different Measures. *Public Administration Review, 63*(5), 586 - 606. https://doi.org/10.1111/1540-6210.00322

Bhimani, A. (2008). Making corporate governance count: the fusion of ethics and economic rationality. *Journal of Management and Governance, 12* (2), 135-147.

Blair, M. (1995). *Ownership and Control: Rethinking Corporate Governance for the Twenty-first Century.* Washington, D.C.: The Brookings Institution. Retrieved on 7 July 2010 from http://www.allianceonline.org/content/index.php?pid=153.

Bleiklie, I., & Kogan, M. (2000). Comparison and Theories. *Transforming Higher Education: A Comparative Study.* London and Philadelphia: Jessica Kingsley.

Boarddevelopment. (n.d.). *Creating a Strong Board Team* Retrieved 13 May 2011 from http://www.boarddevelopment.org/en/1/create_board.aspx

BoardSource. (2005). *Twelve Principles of Governance That Power Exceptional Boards.* Washington, DC: BoardSource.

BoardSource. (2011, November 21). *Definition of Key Terms Used by Nonprofits and their Board of Directors.* Retrieved from http://www.boardsource.org/Knowledge.asp?ID=1.1016.

Brancato, C. K. (1997). *Institutional Investors and Corporate Governance: Best Practices for Increasing Corporate Value.* Chicago: Irwin Professional Publishing.

Cadbury, A. (1992). *Report of the Committee on the Financial Aspects of Corporate Governance.* London: Gee and Co. Ltd.

Carver, J. (1997). Corporate Governance Model from An Unexpected Source—Non-profits. *The Corporate Board,* March/April.

Carver, J. (1997). The Chairperson's Role as Servant Leader of the Board. *The Carver Guide Series on Effective Board Governance, No. 4.* San Francisco, CA: Jossey-Bass.

Carver, J. (1999). The Opportunity in Joint Venture Companies for Re-inventing Corporate Governance. *Corporate Governance - An International Review.*

Carver, J. (1999). The Unique Double Servant-Leadership Role of the Board Chairperson. *Voices of Servant-Leadership Series, No. 2.* Indianapolis: The Robert K. Greenleaf Centre for Servant Leadership.

Carver, J. (2000). *The Policy Governance Model.* Retrieved from http://www.carvergovernance.com/pg-corp.htm

Carver, J. (2006). *Boards That Make a Difference: A new design for leadership in not-for-profit and public organisations.* San Francisco, CA: Jossey-Bass.

Carver, J., & Carver M. (1996). Basic Principles of Policy Governance. *The Carver Guide Series on Effective Board Governance, No. 1.* San Francisco, CA: Jossey-Bass.

Casson, Julia. (no date) *Occasional Paper 8 BY JULIA CASSON A Review of the Ethical Aspects of Corporate Governance Regulation and Guidance in the EU, https://mindleap.co.uk/downloads/areviewoftheethicalaspectsofcorporate governanceregulationandguidanceintheeujune2013.pdf*

Centre for International Private Enterprise (CIPE) (2002). *Instituting Corporate Governance in Developing, Emerging and Transitional Economies.*

Clark, T. (2004). *Theories of Corporate Governance: The Philosophical Foundations of Corporate Governance* London and New York: Routledge as cited in Abdulla, H., & Benedict, V. (2009). Fundamental and Ethics Theories of Corporate Governance. *Middle Eastern Finance and Economics, Issue 4.* Eurojournals Publishing Inc.

Cyert, R. M., & March, J. G. (1963). *A Behaviour Theory of the Firm.* New Jersey-USA, Prentice Hall as cited in Abdulla, H., & Benedict, V. (2009). Fundamental and Ethics Theories of Corporate Governance. *Middle Eastern Finance and Economics, Issue 4.* Eurojournals Publishing Inc.

Cyril, O. H. (1997). *Governing Boards: Their Nature and Nurture.* San Francisco, CA: Jossey-Bass.

Davis, J. H., Schoorman, F. D., & Donaldson, L. (1997). Toward a Stewardship Theory of Management. *Academy of Management Review, 22,* 20-47 as cited in Abdulla, H., & Benedict, V. (2009). Fundamental and Ethics Theories of Corporate Governance. *Middle Eastern Finance and Economics, Issue 4.* Eurojournals Publishing Inc.

De Smet, A., Loch, M., & Schaninger, B. (2007).The Link between Profits and Organisational Performance. *The McKinsey Quarterly.*

Deloitte. (2012). *Developing an effective governance operating model: A guide for financial services boards and management teams* [Ebook]. Retrieved 22 July 2022, from https://www2.deloitte.com/content/dam/Deloitte/global/Documents/Financial-Services/dttl-fsi-US-FSI-Developinganeffectivegovernance-031913.pdf.

Donaldson, T., & Preston, L. E. (1995). The Stakeholder Theory of the Corporation: Concepts, Evidence and Implications. *Academy of Management Review*, Vol. 20, No. 1, pp. 65-91 as cited in Abdulla, H., & Benedict, V. (2009). Fundamental and Ethics Theories of Corporate Governance. *Middle Eastern Finance and Economics, Issue 4*. Eurojournals Publishing Inc.

Donaldson. L., & Davis, J. (1991) Stewardship Theory or Agency Theory: CEO Governance and Shareholder Returns. *Academy Of Management Review*, Vol. 20, No. 1, pp. 65 as cited in Abdulla, H., & Benedict, V. (2009). Fundamental and Ethics Theories of Corporate Governance. *Middle Eastern Finance and Economics, Issue 4*. Eurojournals Publishing Inc.

Drucker, P. F. (1974). *Management: Tasks, Responsibilities, Practices*. New York: HarperCollins.

Economic Rationality. (2009) *Journal of Management and Governance, 12*(2) pp. 135-147 as cited in Abdulla H. & Benedict V. (2009). Fundamental and Ethics Theories of Corporate Governance. *Middle Eastern Finance and Economics, Issue 4*. Eurojournals Publishing Inc.

Forbes. (2007, October 25). *Adam Smith's Folly*. https://www.forbes.com/2007/10/24/adam-smith-corporations-markets-marketsp07-cx_mh_1025hodak.html?sh=1c9eb9ae3c1b

Freeman, R. E. (1999). Response: Divergent Stakeholder Theory. *Academy of Management Review*, 24(2) 233-236 as cited in Abdulla, H., & Benedict, V. (2009). Fundamental and Ethics Theories of Corporate Governance. *Middle Eastern Finance and Economics, Issue 4*. Eurojournals Publishing Inc.

Gayle, D. J., Tewarie, B., & White, A. Q. Jr. (2003). Governance in the twenty-first-century university: Approaches to effective leadership and strategic management. *ERIC Digest*. Retrieved May 9, 2010, from http://www.ericdigests.org/2004-4/governance.htm.

Geneen, H. S. (1984). Why Directors Can't Protect the Shareholders. *Fortune*, 110, 28-29.

Gibendi, R. (10 December 2014). *Top Managers Made Mumias Sugar Lose Over KSh1 Billion, Audit Reveals*. Daily Nation Mobile (Nairobi). Retrieved 4 February 2015.

Gill, M. D. (2005). *Governing for Results: A Director's Guide to Good Governance*. Victoria, BC: Trafford.

Gill, M. (n.d.). *Building Effective Approaches to Governance*. Retrieved from www.snapnonprofit.org/.../BoardGovernance/TypesOfGovernanceModel

Gill, M., & Synergy Associates. (n.d.). *Quick Overview of Governance Models/Board Types*. Retrieved from http://mn.gov/irrb/images/Quick%2520Overview%2520of%2520Governance.pdf

Gillies, J. (1992). *Boardroom Renaissance*. Toronto: McGraw-Hill.

Giorgi, A. (2003, June). *Phenomenology: The philosophy and the method*. Workshop at University of Quebec.

Global Corporate Governance Forum (2005). *Developing Corporate Governance Codes of Best Practice, Toolkit 2*. Washington, DC.: The International Bank for Reconstruction and Development/The World Bank.

Governance and Management Ltd. (2005, April). Determining Board Competences. *Board Matters Newsletter* 4(6).

Hogan, E. (2006). *Governance models.* Retrieved May 13, 2010, from http://site resources.worldbank.org/EDUCATION/Resources/278200-10990 79877269/547664-1099079956815/Global_Trends_University_Governance_webversion.pdf.

IK Vienna School of Governance (n.d.). *Theories and concepts of governance.* Retrieved from https://vigo.univie.ac.at/research/theories-and-concepts-of-governance/

Institute of Governance (2011). *Strengthening Board Governance.* Retrieved May 13, 2011 from http://iog.ca/en/knowledge-areas/board-organizational-governance/strengthening-board-governance.

Institute of Governance (2011). *Why Good Governance Matters.* Retrieved May 13, 2011 from http://iog.ca/en/about-us/governance/why-good-governance-matters.

Iskander, M., & Chamlou, N. (2000). *Corporate governance: a framework for implementation.* Washington, DC: The World Bank.

Kanchinadham, P. (2012, January - March). Corporate Governance: The Strategic Imperative, *Asian Journal of Professional Ethics and Management, 3*(3).

Kaplan, R. S., & Norton, D. P. (1992 January - February). The balanced scorecard: measures that drive performance, *Harvard Business Review,* 71–80.

Laughlin, F. L., & Robert, C. A. (2007). *Good Governance for not-for-profits: developing principles and policies for an effective board.* AMACO.

Leighton, D. S. R., & Thain, D. H. (1997). *Making Boards Work: What Directors Must Do to Make Canadian Boards Effective.* Toronto: McGraw-Hill.

Lipman, F., & Lipman, K. (2006). *Corporate Governance Best Practices: Strategies for Public, private and not-for-profit organisations.* New Jersey: John Wiley & Sons.

Macnamara, D., & Banff Executive Leadership, Inc. (n.d.). *Models of Corporate / Board Governance.* Retrieved from www.banffexeclead.com

Masaoka, J., & Alison, M. (2004). *Why Boards Don't Govern Part 1.* Compass Point Non Profit Services. Retrieved from http://www.compasspoint.org/board-cafe/why-boards-dont-govern-part-1.

McGee, R. W. (Ed.). (2009). *Corporate Governance in Developing Economies.* Miami, FL: Florida International University.

McNamara, C. (n.d.). *Field Guide to Consulting and Organisational Development.* Authenticity Consulting, LLC. Retrieved July 12, 2010 from http://management help.org/org_perf/org_perf.htm.

Michira, M. (2015, February 9). *How Mumias Sugar was Looted Dry.* The Standard. Retrieved from http://www.standardmedia.co.ke/business/article/20001510 62/how-mumias-sugar-was-looted-dry?

Monks, R. A. G., & Minow, N. (1996). Watching the Watchers: Corporate *Governance in the 21st Century.* Cambridge, Mass.: Blackwell.

Monks, R. A., & Minow, N. (2004). *Corporate governance.* Malden, Mass: Blackwell Pub.

Monks, R. A. G, & Minow, N. (2011). *Corporate Governance.* John Wiley & Sons.

OECD (2004). *The Principles of Corporate Governance,* pp. 17-24. Retrieved from http://www.oecd.org/corporate/corporateaffairs/corporategovernanceprinciples/31557724.pdf on date of retrieval

OECD (2005). International Experts Meeting on Corporate Governance of Non-listed Companies. Retrieved from http://www.oecd.org/corporate/ca/corporategovernanceprinciples/35639607.pdf

Private Sector Corporate Governance Trust (n.d.). *Principles for Corporate Governance in Kenya.* Retrieved May 13, 2010 from http://www.ecgi.org/codes/documents/principles_2.pdf

Stahlke, L. (2003). *Governance Matters: Relationship Model of Governance, Leadership and Management.* Canada: GovernanceMatters.com Inc.

Thompson, M., Ellis, R., & Wildawsky, A. (1990). *Cultural Theory.* Boulder.

Todd, A. (n.d.). *Corporate Governance Best Practices: One size does not fit all.* TE Research. Retrieved from http://www.trustenablement.com/local/Corporate_Governance_Practices-One_size_does_not_fit_all.pdf.

Udo, C., B., & Alexander, N., K. (n.d.), *Developments in Corporate Governance.* Retrieved from www.virtusinterpress.org/additional_files/.../sample_chapter01.pdf.

UN. (n.d.). *Good Governance and Human Rights.* Retrieved from http://www.ohchr.org/en/Issues/Development/GoodGovernance/Pages/GoodGovernanceIndex.aspx

Wahito, M. (31 August 2012). *Mumias Profit Drops, Inefficiency To Blame.* 98.4 Capital FM (Nairobi). Retrieved 4 February 2015.

Ward, R. D. (1997). *21ˢᵗ Century Corporate Board.* New York: John Wiley & Sons. Retrieved from www.boardsource.org.

William, A. D. (2006). *Tougher Boards for Tougher Times: Corporate Governance in the Post- Enron Era.* New York: Wiley.

Williamson, O. (1996). *The Mechanisms of Governance.* Oxford: Oxford University Press.

Zimmermann, J. A. M. & Stevens, B. W. (2008). Best practices in board governance: Evidence from South Carolina. *Nonprofit Management and Leadership, 19*: 189–202. doi: 10.1002/nml.218

Further Readings

1. Abdennadher, S., & Cheffi, W. (2020). The effectiveness of E-corporate governance: An exploratory study of internet voting at shareholders' annual meetings in France. *Corporate Governance: The International Journal of Business in Society, 20*(4), 673-702. https://doi.org/10.1108/cg-04-2019-0116

2. Bednar, Michael K. (2012). Watchdog or Lapdog? A Behavioural View of the Media as a Corporate Governance Mechanism. In: *Academy of Management Journal,* 55(1): 131 –150.

3. Benz, Matthias/Frey, Bruno S. (2007). Corporate governance: what can we learn from public governance? In: *Academy of Management Review,* 32(1): 92–104.

4. Charan, A. (2010). E-Governance A New Dimension of Corporate Governance.

5. Jain, S., & Bagga, T. (2021). Role of E-governance in corporate governance and board effectiveness. *2021 9th International Conference on Reliability, Infocom Technologies and Optimization (Trends and Future Directions) (ICRITO).* https://doi.org/10.1109/icrito51393.2021.9596441

6.   Jay Aden Conger, Edward E. Lawler III, David Finegold (2001). Corporate Boards: New Strategies for Adding Value at the Top. Jossy- Bass.

7.   John Harper (2005). *Chairing the Board: A Practical Guide to Activities and Responsibilities.* Kogan Page.

8.   Jonathan R. Macy (2008*). Corporate Governance: Promises Kept, Promises Broken.* Princeton University Press.

9.   Margaret M. Blair (1995). *Ownership and Control: Rethinking Corporate governance for the Twenty-first Century.* Bookings Institution Press.

10.   OECD Report, 2005.

11.   Praptiningsih, M. (2009). Corporate Governance through E-Governance Optimization: a Case Study of Banking Institutions of Indonesia. http://repository.petra.ac.id/15185/1/corporate_governance.pdf

12.   Ram Charan (2005). *Boards that Deliver: Advancing Corporate Governance From Compliance to Competitive Advantage.* Jossey Bass.

13.   Stephen Bainbridge (2008). *The New Corporate Governance in Theory and Practice.* Oxford University Press.

14.   Vasilescu, L. G. (2008). Corporate governance in developing and emerging countries. The case of Romania. *MPRA Paper No. 10998.* Retrieved from http://mpra.ub.uni-muenchen.de/10998/ on July 20, 2010.

15.   Vig, S. (2012). Ensuring Better Corporate Governance through E-Governance. *International Journal of Marketing, Financial Services & Management Research, 1*(9), 188-194.

16.   William A. Dimma (2002). *Excellence in the Boardroom: Best Practices in Corporate Directorship.* John Wiley & Sons.

17.   William G. Bowen (2008). The Board Book: An Insider's Guide for Directors. Norton

18.   www.deloitte.com/us/governanceframework www.corpgov.net/2016/10/the-handbook-of-board-governance

19.   www.strive.com/multimedia/Governance-Excellence-Model-booklet.pdf

Index

integrity, 22, 115–116
  compliance with, 60
intentional board practices, 60
interaction dynamics, 78
internal audit function, 144
internal controls, 149–150
internal corporate governance,
  16–17
internal incentives, 15
internal stakeholders, 5
International Bank for
  Reconstruction and
  Development (IBRD), 114
international corporate
  governance, 8
    inside the firm, 16
    mechanisms, examples of, 16–
    17
International Corporate
  Governance Network, 8
International Development
  Research Centre (IDRC), 94, 96
International Initiatives on
  Corporate Governance, 8
invention, 91

J

Japan Corporate Governance
  Index (JCG Index), 112
Japan Corporate Governance
  Research Institute, 112

K

Kenya National Trading
  Corporation (KNTC), 124
Kenya Wine Agencies Ltd (KWAL),
  124
knowledge management, 57, 94

L

leadership, 10, 50, 74, 91, 150
Leadership Foundation for Higher
  Education (LFHE), 56
learning culture, 92
learning organisation, 94
legal frameworks, 20, 79
liberalisation, 9
line board, 43
linguistic transformation, 29
long-term planning, 94
loyalty, duty of, 49

M

Macnamara and Banff Executive
  Leadership, 44
management, 12, 18–20
board members roles, 48
infrastructure, 78
motivation, 112
revitalization, 138
management by objectives
  (MBOs), 94
management team, 19, 34
marketing boards, 44
market share price, 34
Marshall School of Business
  Centre for Effective
  Organisations, 57
MCA 21 e-Governance Program,
  85
The Modern Corporation and
  Private Property (Berle and
  Means), 7
motivation, 57–58, 91
Mumias Sugar Company case,
  126–128

strategy, governance system, 21–22
supervise organisational operations, 48
supervisory board, 41
support, performance, 92
sustainable development, 10
sustaining resources, 60

T

talent, 22
teamwork, principles of, 55
technology and skills adoption, 76
theories, corporate governance
  agency theory, 26
  argumentative theories, 29
  cultural theory, 29–30
  democratic and legal theory, 30
  gender theory in political science, 30
  political theory, 28–29
  resource dependency theory, 28
  stakeholder theory, 27
  stewardship theory, 26
  transaction cost theory, 28
  transformation and transition theories, 30
time, 58
time-limited organisational strategic plan, 62
top-bottom structure, boards
  board chair, 42
  chief executive officer, 42
  combined CEO-chair, 42
  committees, 42
  inside (executive) directors, 43
  lead director, 43
  shareholders, 42

total quality management (TQM), 94
training, 66
transaction cost theory, 28
Transformational Corporate Leadership (Barine and Minja), 7, 46
transformation and transition theories, 30
transparency, 60, 79, 84, 102, 116
trust building, 89
trustee/pension boards, 44

U

Uchumi Supermarket Ltd., 124–126

W

work environment, 91
working group board, 44
work motivation, 92
World Bank, 6, 8

Z

Zambia Railways Limited (ZRL), 66–69

www.ingramcontent.com/pod-product-compliance
Lightning Source LLC
Chambersburg PA
CBHW071124280326
41935CB00010B/1107